PAGE STREET
PUBLISHING CO.

First published in 2013 by
Page Street Publishing
27 Congress Street, Suite 205-10
Salem, MA 01970
www.pagestreetpublishing.com

Distributed by Macmillan; sales in Canada by The Canadian Manda Group; distribution in Canada by The Jaguar Book Group.

16 15 14 13 1 2 3 4 5

ISBN-13: 978-1-62414-024-2
ISBN-10: 1-62414-024-6

Library of Congress Control Number: 2013934489

Cover and book design by Page Street Publishing
Photography by Tracy Griffith
Photos on pages 4, 6, 10, 38, 62, 64 and 84 by Jill Mortensen

Printed and bound in China

STEALTH HEALTH LUNCHES KIDS LOVE

IRRESISTIBLE AND NUTRITIOUS GLUTEN-FREE SANDWICHES, WRAPS AND OTHER EASY EATS

TRACY GRIFFITH

BESTSELLING AUTHOR OF *SUSHI AMERICAN STYLE*

WITH JILL MORTENSEN

PAGE STREET
PUBLISHING CO.

CONTENTS

INTRODUCTION

Why me and this cookbook? Simply, because I love to cook with kids. And they love it, too. They go bonkers when I teach them how to roll bright Origami Wraps and turn them into kaleidoscopes of tasty fun. The moment a child unwraps his or her first roll is one of sheer, delightful surprise. Always a gasp! Then a clap of buoyant confidence and a little swagger, "Yeah! I made THAT myself! Wanna taste it? Want me to make you one?" Adults have the exact same response, by the way.

As a chef, my professional advice is that if you can get kids to play with their food and have fun creating it, they'll be happier eating it. And eating is always more entertaining when the food's in a roll. All of these recipes involve rolling or stuffing—methods that are easy for kids to do, easy for parents to prep and a fantastic way to sneak in healthy ingredients. Another bonus for Mom and Dad: PRE-paration. Getting everything set to roll before the kids get into the kitchen is easier than ever with my help. Just check out the easy "how-to" photos and tips for make-ahead plans and freeze-for-later foods.

Why did I make these recipes gluten-free? My own experience of going gluten-free (and I do not have celiac disease or gluten intolerance) was life-changing. The increased energy, better concentration and mood lift were remarkable. I got fired up with the challenge of preparing gluten-free gourmet dishes. I also learned that there are so many children who have to avoid gluten, and I felt for them, having to dig a little deeper to sort out their diets in a fast-food, cupcake world. These recipes—every one gluten-free—are fun to make and safe to eat for them and their whole families.

And, hand to heart, I tested over forty kids in three different countries and got pretty much the same reactions everywhere. It usually went like this:

First, the moms would be delighted to have their kids participate. Then they'd show up and immediately begin to apologize: "I'm sorry in advance if Johnny won't eat anything. He's very picky." And, "Please don't think it's your fault if she doesn't like the food." And then, amazed that their picky eaters not only enjoyed their tastings but actually asked for more, they asked for the recipes on the spot. So—not to brag—Stealth Health's food ratings were extremely favorable. I think our kid tasters would have awarded us a couple of mini-Michelin stars.

The other surprise to moms was that they loved the rolls, too. They could tell these bite-sized buddies could do double duty for their own work lunch or cocktail party. They were delighted by how perfect the rolls and wraps are for school lunchboxes but also were thrilled that they pair well with martinis and Pinot Noir!

These recipes were created to be fun, healthy and easy—in that order. They aim to get kids to enjoy cooking, creating and eating new and healthy things. Some recipes might look complicated, but just read through and you'll see that step by step you are going to roll with it. Yes, your first or second roll might be a little chaotic (you know, like your first pancake), but I promise, you and your little guys will find your own rolling rhythm and style.

So, here's to you and your little rockin' rollers: Do your pita thing, fly your wrap flag and get rolling!

TIPS FOR MAKING EASY LUNCHES

WHAT TO MAKE?

Think like a chef. Start off by considering the main event. This is usually the protein (Chicken? Tuna? Cheddar?). Then think about what veggie would taste good with that (kind of like what shoes match this skirt?). There are all sorts of possible combinations: Tuna and cucumbers, chicken and bell peppers, cheddar and ham...

THINK: LEFTOVERS

Have some BBQ chicken? Add some creamy coleslaw under that tangy meat. Extra pork roast? Tuck finely shredded spinach under one of the Stealth Health spreads (such as the sweet bell pepper taste of Red Spread or the pesto yum of Schmoo) that make almost every wrap and roll taste better. They are used repeatedly in this cookbook as foundations of flavor and, of course, covert operators delivering vitamins and nutrition your kid won't see coming. The creamy spreads enhance the other ingredients in every roll, wrap and pocket and are super-concentrated with fresh herbs and vegetables. Your kids might not eat a spoonful of basil and parsley, but with a swipe of Schmoo, consider it done!

HOW TO MAKE IT, OR MIS-YOUR-PLACE, MON CHERI

My best tip? It's in three little French words: *mise-en-place* (set in place). This principle is the key between heaven and Hades for the professional chef, and the same for the home cook. If you get organized before you begin cooking, you will save much time and mental anguish—and you might actually enjoy making food with your kids. *Mise-en-place* is about getting ingredients PREPPED—as in, cleaned, chopped, diced, sliced and measured before you start to cook. Think of it as laying out your outfit for the day. It's so much easier when you get out of the shower and everything you need is all laid out on the bed, right? It's the same with cooking. Also, if your ingredients are pre-cooked and pre-cut, then all the knives are off the counter and it's safe for little hands to be involved. You don't have to stress about what is supposed to be cut into ¼" x 4"/6 x 10 cm pieces now. It's already there in your new best friends: zipper-lock bags.

THE NIGHT BEFORE

The good news about *mise-en-place* is that you can prep a lot of ingredients the night before—sometimes days before, and even while you are cooking another meal. Making a nice salad for dinner? Slice a little more tomato and shred some extra lettuce to pop in little zipper-lock bags, prepped for a quick assembly the next school morning.

THE FRIDGE

Also *mise-en-place* your fridge. Having one shelf designated to your lunch-making section is also a huge mind/time-saver. You don't have to go banging through drawers or rattling past plastic containers to find what you need. Your prepped ingredients will be waiting for you in their tidy bags, as if they're saying, "Hi! Ready to roll!"

WRAP N' FREEZE

Besides making extra sauce, meatloaf or chicken teriyaki that you can freeze to make into wraps later, you'll see which completed wraps and sandwiches are best for freezing. Stuffed pitas are excellent freezing choices, filled with shredded meats, cream cheeses and bell peppers. Burritos, too. Ingredients such as lettuce and tomatoes release a lot of liquid when they thaw and become soggy, so it's best not to include them when freezing. Just thaw out sandwiches in the fridge overnight and simply add fresh vegetables, fruits or pickles—from their shiny bags on their designated shelf in the fridge—in the morning. I recommend double wrapping sandwiches, first with parchment or waxed paper (this is much better than foil, which reacts to acids in foods and can leak micrograms of aluminum into food if it gets warm. For this reason, baking with foil touching food is way out in my book.) Then wrap with plastic wrap or foil to seal against freezer burn and hold the sandwich tight and dripless.

DIPS

Fresh vegetables and chips taste better with dips. And dips can pack a LOT of hidden agents like veggies, garlic and yogurt that do little bodies good. You can freeze dips and salsas in tiny containers—just leave enough room for the liquids to expand when they freeze.

SIDEKICKS

Most of my sandwich and wrap recipes include ideas for complementary sidekicks that really round out your kids' lunchtime. These are homemade chips, crisps, salads and crunchies that can all be made ahead of time and stored in your zipper-lock bags.

CHAPTER ONE

PITA POCKETS

These pockets are perfect stealth health powerhouses. Swipe Red or Golden Spread or Green Dream inside to add more nutrition and help hold in more delicious fillings than a roll or regular sandwich can.

THE HAPS ROLL
HAM AND APPLES WITH SCHMOO

Kids love pesto! And with the sweet crunch of apple combined with melted cheese, this pita is a pleaser every time. These also freeze really well—just wrap in waxed or parchment paper, then plastic wrap, and tuck inside a zipper-lock bag. Presto! Now you are always ready when your kids ask, "Where's 'The HAPS?'"

MAKES 4 PITAS

4 gluten-free pitas (page 39)

½ cup/120 ml Schmoo (page 161)

8 thin slices cheddar cheese

8 slices ham

1 crisp apple, cored and thinly sliced

♥ For each pita, spread 2 tablespoons/30 ml of Schmoo on one side of pita bread with a rubber spatula. Cut cheese and ham to fit the pita's size. Stack from bottom to top a layer of cheese, 2 slices ham, then apple and a final layer of cheese.

♥ Use a Panini press or a large nonstick skillet over medium heat to grill pitas until cheese melts, about 4 minutes per side. Or bake in oven at 300°F/150°C for 3 to 4 minutes, until cheese is melted.

♥ Cut each pita in half. Serve with Bunny Nibbles (page 149), Alligator Scales (page 143) or Zucchini Chips (page 146) and more fresh apple wedges.

CONFETTI POCKETS
ROAST BEEF WITH VEGGIES

With a sly sheet of roast beef, you deliver a whopping amount of protein. The Red Spread covers the four kinds of raw veggies hiding in these pockets with its signature stealth. They'll never know what "healthed" 'em.

MAKES 4 PITAS

2 teaspoons/10 ml olive oil

½ teaspoon/2.5 ml lemon juice

Salt and pepper, to taste

½ cup/75 g carrots, peeled and finely diced

¼ cup/40 g yellow bell peppers, finely diced

¼ cup/40 g red bell peppers, finely diced

¼ cup/40 g English cucumber, seeded and finely diced

4 gluten-free pitas (page 39)

Red Spread (page 156)

½ pound/230 g deli roast beef, sliced wafer thin

♥ Whisk oil and lemon juice together and season with salt and pepper. Toss dressing with carrots, yellow and red bell peppers and cucumbers in a bowl. Set aside.

♥ Split pitas almost all the way open, leaving a "hinge." Spread about 1 tablespoon/15 ml of Red Spread on each pita half. Scatter 1 tablespoon/10 g of dressed veggies on bottom halves and arrange a single layer of roast beef to cover them. Press down on pita firmly. Cut into 4 pieces.

♥ Serve with Origami Crisps (page 140), Sweeties (page 139) or Crunchy Pebbles (page 150).

"I LIKE THE BEEF WITH THE CREAMY CARROT TASTE. AND IT LOOKS LIKE A FIRECRACKER!" —DANIEL, AGE 10

"I LIKE THESE. LIKE YUMMY TURTLE FOOD." —ORLANDO, AGE 6

EMERALD CITY BURGERS
VEGGIE BURGERS IN MINI PITAS

A double dose of cheese helps these green guys go down. Packed with energy-rich beans and mighty spinach, these emerald burgers are just what the great and healthy Oz ordered.

MAKES 4 PITAS

1 16-ounce/450 g can pinto beans, drained and rinsed

½ cup/27.5 g baby spinach leaves

½ cup/75 g rice crumbs

½ cup/45 g cheddar cheese, finely grated

½ cup/75 g finely grated carrots (about 2 medium carrots)

1 scallion, finely chopped

1 large egg, lightly beaten

Kosher salt and ground pepper, to taste

1 tablespoon/15 ml olive oil

4 ounces/113 g mozzarella cheese, shredded

4 gluten-free mini pitas

Green Slime (page 158) for serving

Alfalfa sprouts, for topping (optional)

♥ In a food processor, briefly pulse the pinto beans and the spinach. Then add rice crumbs, cheddar cheese, carrots, scallion and egg, and pulse briefly again. Pour out into a bowl and season with salt and pepper, mixing with your hands. Form 8 small 3-inch/7.6 cm patties.

♥ In a large skillet, heat olive oil over medium heat. Fry veggie patties, pressing lightly to flatten, until browned—about 3 minutes. Flip burgers, sprinkle mozzarella on tops and cook another 3 minutes.

♥ Warm pitas, slice almost to the end and swipe a little Green Slime inside both pita sides. Tuck in a warm burger, and stuff in a couple of sprouts if you can!

♥ Serve with Bunny Nibbles (page 149) or Origami Crisps (page 140).

CHICKEN LITTLE POCKETS

EGG SALAD PITAS

Feed your chicken littles these sunny pockets packed with delicious eggs—a rich source of amino acids that allow easy absorption of proteins for growing bodies. With the delightful cleansing crunch of celery, all tucked into a creamy jacket of Red or Golden Spread, these pockets will always please.

MAKES 4 PITAS

6 eggs

Water and ice for ice bath

¼ cup/60 g mayonnaise

2 teaspoons/10 g Dijon mustard

2 teaspoons/10 ml lemon juice

½ stalk celery, finely chopped, about 3 tablespoons/30 g (optional)

¼ teaspoon salt

Freshly ground black pepper, to taste

4 gluten-free pitas (page 39)

¼ cup/60 ml Red Spread (page 156), Golden Spread (page 162) or Green Dream (page 159)

♥ Place eggs in medium saucepan, cover with 1 inch/2.5 cm of water, and bring to boil over medium heat. Remove pan from heat, cover, and let eggs sit in hot water for 10 minutes. Meanwhile, fill a medium bowl with 4 cups/950 ml of water and 1 tray of ice cubes. Transfer eggs to ice water bath and let sit 5 minutes (this keeps the yolks from getting green around the edges and sliming your egg salad color). Peel cooled eggs and chop to a medium dice.

♥ Mix eggs, mayonnaise, mustard, lemon juice, celery (if using), salt and pepper together in medium bowl. Can be covered and refrigerated overnight.

♥ Slice pita almost to end. Swipe inside tops and bottoms of pitas with 1 tablespoon/15 ml of your choice of spread and stuff with egg salad.

♥ Serve with Bunny Nibbles (page 149), Origami Crisps (page 140), sweet pickles or apple slices.

SLOPPY T-JOES
TURKEY SLOPPY JOES

Who doesn't love Sloppy Joes? Made with lean turkey and gluten-free pitas, this Sloppy will give your little Joes lots of good protein and energy. Feel free to make the turkey mixture in a slow cooker—cook on medium-high for 2 hours. These Joes freeze well double-wrapped in parchment and then plastic wrap.

MAKES 8 PITAS

2 tablespoons/30 ml olive oil

1 small onion, finely chopped

2 medium-size carrots, finely grated, about 1½ cups/165 g

1 clove garlic, pressed

2 pounds/900 g ground light and dark turkey meat

1 tablespoon/45 g tomato paste

½ cup/120 ml water

½ cup/120 g ketchup

¼ cup/45 g packed brown sugar

1 tablespoon/15 ml cider vinegar

1 tablespoon/11 g yellow mustard

½ teaspoon salt

¼ cup/30 g gluten-free, all-purpose flour

½ cup/120 ml of Red Spread (page 156), Green Dream (page 159) or Golden Spread (page 162)

1 cup/47 g shredded lettuce

8 gluten-free pitas (page 39)

♥ In a large skillet, heat olive oil over medium-high heat and sauté onion, carrot and garlic about 5 minutes. Add turkey meat and sauté until no longer pink, about 4 to 5 minutes. Stir in tomato paste, water, ketchup, brown sugar, cider vinegar, mustard and salt, and stir well. Reduce heat to medium-low and cover and cook for 20 minutes more, stirring occasionally. Remove from heat and let cool.

♥ For each pita, pry open pita leaving a connecting hinge and swipe insides with your choice of spread. Tuck in a bit of shredded lettuce then stuff with Sloppy T-Joe mixture.

♥ Serve with Sweeties (page 139), Origami Crisps (page 140) or Alligator Scales (page 143).

THE LORAX

TURKEY WITH SWISS AND GRAPES

Let the Lorax speak for the joy of grapes and turkey! Sweet and savory always make a taste-bud party, and grapes, beloved by most kids, are fresher than the usual combo of cranberry with turkey. This recipe is very flexible—you can change it up with different cheeses, such as cheddar or mozzarella, and try it with ham or chopped-up sausage. Another great option is making a few and freezing for those busy school-day mornings.

MAKES 4 PITAS

½ cup/120 ml Schmoo (page 161), Red Spread (page 156) or Golden Spread (page 162)

4 gluten-free pitas (page 39)

8 slices Swiss cheese

8 slices deli turkey

¼ cup/40 g red or green seedless grapes, halved

♥ Spread 2 tablespoons/30 ml of Schmoo (or Red Spread or Golden Spread) inside each pita bread with a rubber spatula. Cut cheese and turkey to fit the pita's size. Press some grape halves into the spread. Then layer a slice of cheese, then turkey, and repeat the layers. Make the rest of the pitas in the same way.

♥ Using a panini press or a large nonstick skillet over medium heat, grill pitas until cheese melts, about 4 minutes per side. Or bake in oven at 300°F/150°C for 3 to 4 minutes, until cheese is melted. Cut each pita in half. If freezing, let cool completely and wrap with parchment paper and foil. Let thaw overnight and heat in 350°F/177°C oven for 10 minutes before packing in lunchbox the next morning.

♥ Serve with Bunny Nibbles (page 149), Alligator Scales (page 143) or Zucchini Chips (page 146) and fresh apple wedges.

"ONE OF MY FAVORITES. YOU COULD CALL IT 'THE FRUITY PATOOTIE.'"
—LUCCA, AGE 10

FRUITY PATOOTIE POCKETS
CHICKEN, GRAPES, APPLES AND PEANUT BUTTER

What is it about peanut butter? Whatever you toss with it, there it goes! Peanut butter might taste great, but it also packs serious vitamin B6 for healthy blood cells and vitamin A for eyes. It's also high in "good" fat. So let your little ones Fruity Patootie at least twice a week.

MAKES 4 PITAS

½ cup/130 g crunchy peanut butter

2 tablespoons/30 g mayonnaise

2 tablespoons/30 ml honey

2 cups/250 g cooked chicken breast, shredded

½ cup/40 g green or red grapes, roughly chopped

1 crisp apple, cored and thinly sliced

♥ In a medium bowl, mix peanut butter, mayonnaise and honey to combine well. Toss mixture with chicken and grapes. Spoon into whole pitas. Slip in a few slices of apple on top of the chicken mixture.

♥ Serve with Bunny Nibbles (page 149) or Origami Crisps (page 140).

HELLO KITTY ROLL
SALMON CUCUMBER SANDWICH WITH GREEN DREAM

These lovely pastel pinwheels are packed with super salmon and cool cucumber. These whirlies are excellent choices for freezing as well. Rolling these up like little pinwheels gives a different look from a plain old stuffed pita.

MAKES 4 PINWHEELS

2 gluten-free pitas, split open (page 39)

½ cup/120 ml Green Dream (page 159)

½ cup/75 g English cucumber, very thinly sliced on mandolin

6 ounces/170 g boneless cooked salmon or smoked salmon, sliced wafer-thin

♥ For each pita, spread Green Dream to cover the inside. Leaving a ½-inch/1.3-cm border all around the edges, place cucumber slices over Green Dream, then lay several wafer-thin layers of salmon over the cucumbers.

♥ Crimp the lower pita edge and then roll tightly forward like you're rolling up a magazine. Let the pinwheeled pita rest on the seam while you repeat rolling the remaining pitas. Cut in half on the diagonal to make 4 pinwheels, or cut into even pieces for smaller pinwheels.

♥ Serve with a sidekick of Hearts and Stars (page 134) and Origami Crisps (page 140), Crunchy Pebbles (page 150) or Sharky Chips (page 145).

"I WANT MORE—I LOVE IT. MOMMY, PLEASE GET THE RECIPE!"
—GARRETT, AGE 9

HAM AND CHEESE TOASTIES
TOASTED HAM AND CHEESE WITH APPLES

I made this classic sandwich healthy with a surprise crunch of fresh, sweet apple. Schmoo packs hidden fresh herb and spinach goodness, and the Red Spread is loaded with nutritious sweet peppers. Seems whatever these veggie-packed cream cheeses are spread on gets eaten up by little mouths. These toasties also work great with gluten-free bagels substituted for the pitas.

MAKES 4 PITAS

4–6 thin slices ham

4–8 slices cheddar cheese, depending on desired cheesiness

4 gluten-free pitas (page 39)

4 tablespoons/60 ml Schmoo (page 161) or Red Spread (page 156)

½ green apple, cored and sliced wafer-thin

1½ medium tomatoes, thinly sliced into 12–14 slices

2 tablespoons/30 g unsalted butter

♥ Trim ham and cheese slices into rounds to fit pitas.

♥ For each pita, slit pita in half and spread insides with Schmoo or Red Spread. Layer a single slice of cheese, 4 slices of apple, 3 slices tomato, 1 or 1½ slices ham, and finish with another layer of cheese, if desired. Top each with remaining pita halves.

♥ Press pitas in a Panini press or melt butter in a large skillet and carefully place the 4 pitas in the butter. Top with a heavy pot to press, and cook for about 2 minutes each side. Remove from press or skillet when cheese is melted. Cut pitas in half to serve.

♥ Serve with fresh apple slices.

THE WOLVERINE
TURKEY MEATLOAF SANDWICH

Why turkey? It's a real covert operation in stealth health with less fat than traditional pork and beef. Hidden carrots, Red Spread packed with vitamins and calcium, and the mineral-rich maple syrup all make this sandwich super healthy. This is one wolverine you will want to keep around the house. Meatloaf can be dinner the night before so you only have to prep and cook once for this pita's fixings.

MAKES 4 PITAS

2 large carrots, peeled and finely shredded

1 pound/450 g ground, mixed dark and white turkey meat

½ cup/75 g rice crumbs

2 tablespoons + 3 teaspoons/ 45 ml teriyaki sauce, divided

1 tablespoon/11 g yellow mustard

⅔ cup/160 ml Vampire Sauce, divided (see page 165)

3 tablespoons/45 ml maple syrup

1 teaspoon/6.7 g salt

1 teaspoon/6.7 g black pepper

4 gluten-free pitas (page 39)

½ cup/128 g Red Spread (page 156)

1 cup/55 g finely shredded green leaf lettuce

♥ Preheat oven to 350°F/177°C.

♥ In a large bowl, use your hands to mix together the carrots, turkey, rice crumbs, 2 tablespoons/30 ml teriyaki sauce, the mustard, ⅓ cup/80 ml of the Vampire Sauce, 1 tablespoon/15 ml of the maple syrup, the salt and black pepper.

♥ Gently shape the mixture into a plump loaf and place in a greased loaf pan. Don't pack the meat too tightly or you'll have some tough turkey.

♥ In a small bowl, whisk together the remaining 3 teaspoons/15 ml teriyaki sauce, ⅓ cup/80 ml Vampire Sauce and 2 tablespoons/30 ml maple syrup. Spread this mixture evenly all over the top of the turkey loaf. Bake for 40 minutes. Let cool, then slice into ½-inch/1.3-cm slices.

♥ Split each pita and spread 1 tablespoon/15 ml of Red Spread on each half. On each bottom half, arrange ¼ cup/14 g shredded lettuce. Top with meatloaf slices to cover the lettuce. Top with other half of the pita and press to close. Cut in half and serve with green grapes, Bunny Nibbles (page 149) or Origami Crisps (page 140) for a great lunchbox.

STRAWBERRIES AND CREAM
FRESH STRAWBERRIES, PEANUT BUTTER AND CREAM CHEESE PITAS

A livelier take on the old PBJ standard with the nutritional goodness of fresh fruit and calcium from the cream cheese, and without the extra sugar of prepared jams. Wrap up slices with waxed paper and foil for an easy lunch-box favorite that will be popular as an after-school snack, too.

MAKES 2 PITAS

2 gluten-free pitas (page 39)

4 tablespoons/60 g natural peanut butter

4 tablespoons/60 ml whipped cream cheese

16 medium strawberries, roughly chopped

♥ Split each pita open and spread whipped cream cheese on one half and peanut butter on the other. Press some chopped strawberries onto cream cheese side and top strawberries with peanut butter side. Cut pita into quarters to serve. Send your little ones off with Origami Crisps (page 140) and extra strawberries.

CHICKI-YAKI

CHICKEN TERIYAKI WITH CUCUMBER CREAM CHEESE

This flavorsome chicki is sooo good, be sure to make enough so you can keep some leftovers for the next day's lunch. Sweet, salty and gingery meat combined with creamy cream cheese and cucumber. Oh! This chicki knows how to rock her pita pocket.

MAKES 4 PITAS

½ cup/120 ml honey

2 tablespoons/30 ml rice vinegar

2 tablespoons/30 ml soy sauce

2 cloves garlic, pressed

1 tablespoon/8 g peeled and finely grated fresh ginger

Kosher salt and ground pepper

4–5 boneless, skin-on chicken thighs (about 2 pounds/910 g)

½ English cucumber, seeded and coarsely grated

¼ teaspoon seasoned rice vinegar

1 cup/240 ml whipped cream cheese

2 tablespoons/30 ml canola oil

4 gluten-free pitas (page 39)

♥ In a large bowl, mix honey, vinegar, soy sauce, garlic, ginger, 1 tablespoon/20 g Kosher salt and ½ teaspoon pepper. Add chicken and toss to coat. Let marinate for at least 1 hour and up to 8 hours.

♥ Put grated cucumber in a mesh sieve and lightly toss with a few pinches of salt. This will release a lot of water. Let drain for 15 minutes, then place the cucumber into a double layer of paper towels, twist into a ball and squeeze out water. Mix the cucumbers with the seasoned rice vinegar and cream cheese and chill for about 30 minutes or up to 3 days ahead.

♥ Heat oil in a grill pan over medium-high heat. Drain chicken from marinade, wiping a little off with paper towels, and lay skin-side down in grill pan. Cook about 5 to 6 minutes without disturbing to get a good sear on (*yaki* means "grilled" in Japanese). Flip chicken over and grill another 4 to 5 minutes. Remove to a cutting board and let cool 5 minutes. Cut into ¼-inch/0.6-cm strips and use immediately for pitas or keep in an airtight container up to 3 days.

♥ Swipe insides of pitas with the cucumber cream cheese then stuff with chicki-yaki slices. Wrap the pitas in parchment and plastic wrap and send your kids off with sidekicks of Bunny Nibbles (page 149), Sweeties (page 139) or Origami Crisps (page 140). These pitas are also great with Hearts and Stars (page 134).

. . . .

This yummy cucumber dip is delicious with almost all chips, crisps or fresh veggie sticks.

TURKEY SNAP ROLL
TURKEY, CUCUMBER AND SCHMOO

Simple and tasty with a clean, invigorating cucumber crunch, and protein and calcium-rich, this pita is no turkey. It also freezes very well, so make extra and don't forget you did!

MAKES 4 PITAS

4 gluten-free pitas (page 39)

½ cup (120 ml) Schmoo (page 161) or Red Spread (page 156)

½ English cucumber, thinly sliced

8 thin slices turkey

♥ Split each pita almost all the way, leaving a hinge, and spread Schmoo on upper and lower insides of pocket. Tuck in a few cucumbers into the Schmoo. Then tuck in some turkey slices and wrap it up. Serve with sidekicks of Crunchy Pebbles (page 150) and Origami Crisps (page 140).

"YOU SHOULD CALL IT 'JUST ONE MORE BITE.'"
—VERA, AGE 4

MANGA BURGERS
SALMON TERIYAKI BURGERS

Lovely pink salmon is rich with omega-3s and vitamin D to soothe inflammation and boost the immune system. With a warm, golden crust and cool cucumber snap, this pita pocket is the best of both food worlds.

6 SMALL BURGERS IN MINI-PITAS

½ **English cucumber, thinly sliced**

1 tablespoon/15 ml **seasoned rice vinegar**

1 **egg**

2 tablespoons/30 ml **teriyaki sauce, divided**

1½ cups/337 g **cooked salmon fillet, flaked**

½ cup/75 g **rice crumbs**

2 **scallions, finely chopped**

Pinch of salt and a pinch of pepper

2 teaspoons/10 g **butter**

1 teaspoon/5 ml **olive oil**

6 **mini gluten-free pitas (page 39)**

¼ cup/60 ml **Red Spread (page 156)**

♥ In a bowl, toss cucumber with vinegar, and set aside to marinate while you make the salmon burgers.

♥ In another bowl, whisk together egg and 1 tablespoon/15 ml teriyaki sauce. Mix in salmon, rice crumbs and scallions, kneading with your hands. Form into six 3-inch/7.6-cm patties, ½ inch/1.3 cm thick.

♥ Drain cucumbers and turn out on a paper towel to dry off. Put the remaining 1 tablespoon/15 ml teriyaki sauce in a small bowl and have a BBQ brush standing by.

♥ In a large skillet, heat butter and oil over moderately high heat until hot. Add patties and fry on each side for about 2 minutes. Brush tops of patties with a little teriyaki sauce and cover pan to cook 2 more minutes.

♥ Split pitas and warm in a toaster oven for 3 minutes. Swipe a thin layer of Red Spread on each side. Arrange cucumber slices around bottom halves of pitas. Top with a Manga Burger, then with other pita halves.

♥ Serve with Hearts and Stars (page 134) and Sharky Chips (page 145) with Red Spread and/or Green Slime (page 158). Yum!

GLUTEN-FREE PITAS

These gluten-free pitas are so tasty you won't miss gluten or store-bought pitas ever again. Make a double batch and freeze half the booty. Also, filled pita sandwiches freeze extremely well (just leave off the tomato or lettuce until ready to serve).

MAKES 6 MINI PITAS

1 cup/120 g all-purpose, gluten-free flour

½ cup/60 g millet flour

½ cup/60 g brown rice flour

¼ cup /60 g ground flaxseed

1 teaspoon/2.5 g xanthan gum

1½ teaspoons/6.9 g baking soda

¼ teaspoon cream of tartar

1 teaspoon/6.7 g Kosher salt

¼ cup/60 ml warm water

2 eggs

2 teaspoons/10 ml olive oil

¾–1 cup/180–240 ml warm water

♥ Preheat oven to 400°F/204°C with a pizza stone in the oven. If you don't have a pizza stone, turn your sturdiest baking sheet upside down and preheat that.

♥ In a large bowl, whisk together the flours, flaxseed, xanthan gum, baking soda, cream of tartar and salt.

♥ In a separate bowl, whisk together ¼ cup/60 ml warm water, eggs and olive oil. Add this wet mixture to the dry mixture. Then slowly add another ½ cup/120 ml of warm water, mixing to make a wet dough until dough pulls away from the side of the bowl. Scrape dough out onto a damp cutting board and divide into 6 equal parts. Ready a sheet of parchment paper on work surface.

♥ With wet hands, pull a handful of dough onto a sheet of parchment paper and smooth into a ½-inch/1.3-cm thick round about 3 inches/7.6 cm wide. Repeat with the remaining pieces of dough to get 6 even pieces and place about ½ inch/1.3 cm apart on the parchment paper. Place the parchment paper on the hot pizza stone or baking sheet.

♥ Bake for 5 to 6 minutes, then carefully flip pitas and bake for another 5 to 7 minutes, or until lightly brown on both sides. Allow to cool for 5 minutes.

♥ Slice each round almost in half, leaving a connecting hinge on each. With a very sharp knife, gently coax open the center of each pita half.

♥ Once cooled, the pitas will keep for 2 days in a plastic zipper-lock bag at room temperature.

CHAPTER TWO

TACOS AND TORTILLAS

Tacos and tortillas always add some olé to your lunch, but none can compare to the Stealth Health–wrapped goodness these recipes roll to you and your niños. They are easy to stuff, roll and pack for fun school lunches. For gluten-free tacos and tortillas, make sure the taco shells and tortillas you purchase are made with 100% corn flour and none of the wheat that some producers use.

TOM TACOS
TURKEY TACOS

Crunchy tacos without gluten or heavy beef—these Toms give your tacos a healthy olé! For school lunches, pack the turkey in one little container and the taco shells in another. The toppings can travel in small baggies, and your little mariachis can make their own taco treats on the spot.

MAKES 10 CRISPY TACOS

2 tablespoons/30 ml olive oil

¾ cup/110 g onion, chopped medium

1 pound/450 g ground turkey (dark and light meat)

1 tablespoon/15 g chili powder

1 teaspoon/3.3 g coarse salt

1 tablespoon/16 g tomato paste

1 cup/240 ml chicken broth or water

10 gluten-free crispy taco shells

6 ounces/150 g shredded Monterey Jack and cheddar cheese blend

½ head iceberg lettuce, finely shredded

1 medium red tomato, diced

Toppings: Green Slime (page 158), salsa, sour cream

♥ Heat oil in a large sauté pan over medium-high heat. When oil shimmers, add onion and cook until onion becomes translucent, about 4 minutes. Add turkey and cook just until meat is cooked through, 3 to 4 minutes.

♥ Stir in chili powder, salt, tomato paste and broth and simmer, stirring occasionally, until thickened, about 10 minutes. Remove from heat.

♥ Fill each taco shell with desired amounts of turkey, cheese, lettuce and tomato. Top with your favorite toppings like Green Slime, salsa, and sour cream or plain yogurt.

♥ Serve with Hearts and Stars (page 134).

CHINESE CHICKEN ROLLS
CHICKEN, SCALLIONS, CUCUMBERS AND HOISIN SAUCE

Mmmmm, sweet and tangy hoisin, salt and pepper chicken and clean cucumber crunching through. An excellent Asian version of BBQ chicken, this roll shines in gluten-free tortillas. Of course, any leftover chicken works well with this. Use Crispy Rice Noodles (page 135) instead of peanuts if you're allergic.

MAKES 4 TORTILLAS

4 boneless, skinless chicken thighs

1 tablespoon/20 g Kosher salt

Freshly ground black pepper, to taste

2 tablespoons/30 ml olive oil

4 gluten-free tortillas (page 63)

½ cup/120 ml Red Spread (page 156) or Golden Spread (page 162)

½ cup/120 ml hoisin sauce

½ cup/75 g roasted, salted peanuts or almonds, chopped (optional)

6 scallions

½ English cucumber

♥ Season both sides of the chicken thighs with salt and pepper and set aside in a bowl while you prep the vegetables.

♥ Trim the scallions and split them lengthwise. Seed the cucumber and cut into ¼" x 4"/0.6 x 10 cm sticks.

♥ Heat olive oil in a grill pan on medium-high. Grill thighs about 7 to 8 minutes. Turn thighs over and keep grilling for another 7 to 8 minutes. Remove from pan and let cool. Slice thighs lengthwise into ½-inch/1.3-cm strips.

♥ Lay a tortilla down on work surface. Swipe a thin layer of Red or Golden Spread across middle of tortilla. Dab about 1 teaspoon/5 ml of hoisin sauce over spread. Sprinkle a couple of teaspoons of peanuts (if using). Place scallions and cucumber over peanuts, then top with strips of chicken, letting all ingredients reach to the ends of the tortilla. Roll bottom edge of tortilla up and around ingredients, grasp tightly and then roll up into a snug roll. Repeat with remaining ingredients.

♥ Cut on the diagonal and serve with extra hoisin sauce for dipping and with Hearts and Stars (page 134), Origami Crisps (page 140) or Crunchy Pebbles (page 150).

FISH STIX TACOS
HOMEMADE FISH STICKS WITH CITRUS SLAW

You can use tilapia or codfish to make these delicious fish sticks. Kids seem to love any fish that's golden fried. Of course, substitute your favorite prepared fish sticks if you're crunched for time. The fresh toppings carry a wallop of veggie nutrition, and no one can eat just one.

MAKES 8 TACOS

½ cup/120 ml buttermilk

Salt and pepper, to taste

2½ pounds/1130 g tilapia or codfish fillets, cut into 4" x 2"/10 x 5 cm strips

½ cup/120 ml Red Spread (page 156) or Golden Spread (page 162)

1 cup/55 g thinly shredded Napa cabbage

1 carrot, finely grated

2 large eggs, beaten

1 tablespoon/15 ml milk

½ cup/60 g rice flour

1 ½ cups/225 g rice crumbs

1 ½ cups/350 ml canola oil, plus more if needed

8 small gluten-free taco shells

♥ Season buttermilk with a little salt and pinch or two of pepper. Put fish filets in a bowl with seasoned buttermilk and let soak for about 10 to 15 minutes while you make the slaw. This takes out any fishy taste and plumps up the fish.

♥ In a medium bowl, mix together the Red or Golden Spread with the cabbage and carrots to make a coleslaw.

♥ Whisk eggs and milk together. Put flour, egg mixture and rice crumbs each in separate bowls. Place the fish filets one at a time into the flour bowl and dust thoroughly. Dip dusted filet in egg mixture, then roll in rice crumbs.

♥ Heat the oil in a large nonstick skillet over medium-high heat. Cook the fish filets in batches until crispy and golden, about 2 to 3 minutes per side.

♥ Dollop about 1 tablespoon/15 ml of the Golden Spread coleslaw in the bottom and side of each taco shell. Top with fish stix and serve with your favorite salsa or some Vampire Sauce (page 165), if desired.

ALOHA TORTILLAS
GRILLED PORK AND PINEAPPLE ROLLS

Pineapples are rich in vitamins A and C, which will help your child fight off colds. Kids will love the sweet flavor and crispy texture of this taco. (And Mommy and Daddy will, too. Cocktail canapés, anyone?) Set out all the ingredients and let your kids build and roll their own tortillas. These are just as great as tacos.

MAKES 6 TORTILLAS

2 tablespoons/23 g brown sugar

2 teaspoons/13.3 g Kosher salt

½ teaspoon cinnamon

1 pound/450 g pork tenderloin

1 tablespoon/15 ml olive oil

½ cup/120 ml Red Spread (page 156) or Golden Spread (page 162)

½ cup/120 ml Green Slime (page 158)

2 cups/100 g finely shredded green lettuce (optional)

¼ fresh pineapple, cored, skinned and cut into ½"/1.3 cm slices

6 gluten-free tortillas (page 63)

♥ In a small bowl, combine brown sugar, salt and cinnamon. Rub over pork tenderloin, wrap in plastic wrap and refrigerate overnight. (Or use leftover pork, thinly sliced or shredded.)

♥ Heat olive oil in a grill pan over medium heat. Grill pork, cooking on all sides for about 3 to 4 minutes each side. Remove pork and set aside on cutting board. Keeping heat on medium under pan, throw on pineapple slices in batches to grill for about 2 minutes on each side. Cut grilled pork and pineapple into 4" x ⅛"/10 x 0.3 cm sticks.

♥ For each tortilla, swipe 1 tablespoon/15 ml of Red Spread then 1 tablespoon/15 ml of Green Slime on lower third of tortilla. Scatter some shredded lettuce over Slime. Top with triple strips of pork and double sticks of pineapple.

♥ Roll bottom edge of tortilla up and around ingredients, grasp tightly and then roll up into a snug roll. Cut on the diagonal. Repeat with remaining ingredients.

♥ Serve with Crunchy Pebbles (page 150) and some extra Green Slime for dipping.

"AI CARAMBA!" WRAP
GRILLED CHICKEN WITH GREEN SLIME

Any kind of leftover cooked chicken or pork will work well with this wrap. The Green Slime packs the super-food power of avocado and herb in every tablespoon. This perfect lunch-box staple only gets better as the flavors meld together. You can also swap out the tortilla for a Mango Gem Wrap and add a bit of rice for a super-deluxe and delicious burrito.

MAKES 4 WRAPS

4 8"/20 cm gluten-free tortillas (page 63)

2 tablespoons/30 ml Green Slime (page 158)

2 cups/180 g shredded Monterey Jack cheese

4 cups/220 g shredded green leaf lettuce (like Romaine or Butter)

½ cup/75 g tomato, seeded and chopped

2 cups/280 g shredded, cooked chicken

♥ Lay one tortilla on a work surface. If making a burrito, press about 2 tablespoons/26 g of cooked rice in a neat rectangle in center of tortilla or Gem Wrap.

♥ Spread 2 tablespoons/30 ml of Green Slime over tortilla, leaving a 2"/5 cm bare border all around. Sprinkle cheese over Green Slime. Sprinkle shredded lettuce over cheese. Scatter tomatoes on top of lettuce. Place about 2½ ounces/70 g of chicken in an even line across the center of the tomatoes.

♥ Roll bottom edge of tortilla up and around ingredients, grasp tightly and then roll up into a snug roll. Cut on the diagonal. Repeat with remaining ingredients.

♥ Wraps can be made the night before—wrap in parchment paper, then plastic wrap and refrigerate.

CHICKADILLAS

CHICKEN QUESADILLAS WITH BLACK BEANS AND AVOCADO SALSA

Anything with melted cheese is good. Adding potassium-packed avocados, antioxidant-rich tomatoes, and black beans makes these quesadillas good for all kids great and small. This recipe also freezes well, so make a bunch and double wrap in parchment and plastic wrap to pop in the freezer.

MAKES 8 SMALL QUESADILLAS

BLACK BEAN PASTE

1 ½ cups/420 g cooked black beans, drained (or 1 15-ounce/420 g can)

¼ small, sweet onion, chopped

1 small clove garlic, pressed

2 teaspoons (10 ml) lime juice

⅛ teaspoon cumin

¼ teaspoon salt

AVOCADO SALSA

2 scallions, finely chopped

2 plum tomatoes, finely chopped

½ small clove garlic, pressed

1 tablespoon/1 g finely chopped cilantro (optional)

1 teaspoon/6.7 g salt

2 avocados, diced medium

Juice of ½ lime

8 small, gluten-free, corn tortillas

¾ cup/168 g sour cream or plain yogurt

1 cup/90 g shredded cheddar and/or Monterey Jack cheese

2 cups/280 g shredded, cooked chicken

FOR BLACK BEAN PASTE:

♥ Pulse all ingredients in a food processor or blender to a paste. Set aside.

FOR AVOCADO SALSA:

♥ Place all ingredients in a small bowl and gently stir to mix.

FOR EACH QUESADILLA:

♥ Spread a thin layer of Black Bean Paste over the tortilla, leaving a 1-inch/2.5 cm border bare. On one half of the Black Bean Paste circle, smear 1 generous tablespoon/18 g of sour cream, then sprinkle 2 tablespoons/11 g of cheese. Follow with about 4 tablespoons/35 g of shredded chicken and 2 teaspoons/10.4 g of Avocado Salsa. Fold the tortilla in half and press down to close. Repeat with remaining ingredients.

♥ Heat a dry, ridged griddle pan. Place folded tortilla on griddle pan and heat for 3 minutes. Flip tortilla and cook on the other side for 2 minutes.

♥ Serve with extra Avocado Salsa and sour cream, if desired.

UNICORN ROLL
CRISPY CHICKEN FINGERS AND APPLES

These crunchy chicken and apple rolls look like horns but taste so good! From helping keep your teeth clean to deliciously providing soluble fiber, no wonder an apple a day keeps the doctor away.

MAKES 4 ROLLS

½ cup/120 ml bottled sweet Thai chili sauce, plus more for dipping

8 tablespoons/113 g (1 stick) unsalted butter, melted

1 teaspoon/6.7 g sea salt

1 Granny Smith apple, peeled, cored and cut into 16 thin wedges

1 pound/450 g skinless, boneless chicken breast halves

3½ cups/100 g cornflakes, coarsely crushed

4 gluten-free tortillas (page 63)

8 tablespoons/120 ml Red Spread (page 156) or Golden Spread (page 162)

1 cup/55 g shredded green leaf lettuce

♥ Preheat oven to 425°F/232°C. Place one baking rack in the top third of the oven and one in the lower third.

♥ In a small saucepan over low, heat sweet Thai chili sauce until warm, about 3 minutes. Remove from heat and whisk in butter and salt. Set glaze aside in pan.

♥ In a medium bowl, toss apples with 2 tablespoons/30 ml of the glaze. Arrange in a single layer on a greased baking sheet. Set aside.

♥ Butter a 9" x 13" /23 x 33 cm baking dish.

♥ Pour cornflakes into a shallow dish. Cut chicken lengthwise into ½-inch/ 1.3-cm strips. Dip one chicken strip at a time into remaining butter glaze, then dredge in cornflakes, pressing firmly. Transfer coated strips to buttered baking dish.

♥ Place chicken dish on top oven rack and apples on lower oven rack. Bake until chicken is golden and apples are lightly baked, turning pans around halfway through cooking, about 15 to 20 minutes total. Cool chicken strips and apple wedges in pans to room temperature. Sprinkle with a little additional sea salt.

♥ Place tortillas in oven or toaster to warm for a few minutes just before use. Place one tortilla on work surface and spread about 2 tablespoons/ 30 ml of Red Spread evenly over tortilla. Scatter lettuce over spread. Place 2 to 3 chicken strips and 4 apple wedges across lower third of tortilla. Roll bottom edge of tortilla up and around ingredients, grasp tightly and then roll up into a snug roll. Cut on the diagonal. Repeat with remaining ingredients.

MEXICALI ROLLS
CHICKEN FAJITAS

Sweet onion and peppers, seared marinated chicken and the double goodness of Red Spread and Green Slime, all rolled in tender tortillas. These mighty Mexicalis can be rolled, wrapped and frozen.

MAKES 6 FAJITAS

2 pounds/900 g skinless, boneless chicken breasts

2 tablespoons/30 ml lime juice

3 tablespoons/45 ml olive oil

1 clove garlic, pressed

1 tablespoon/20 g salt

½ teaspoon chili powder

2 tablespoons/30 ml canola or safflower oil

1 large sweet onion (such as Vidalia or Walla Walla), cut lengthwise into ¼"/0.6 cm slices

3 bell peppers (red, yellow and orange), sliced lengthwise into ¼"/0.6 cm strips

1 teaspoon/6.7 g salt

Freshly ground pepper, to taste

8–10 gluten-free tortillas (page 63)

1 cup/240 ml Red Spread (page 156)

½ cup/120 ml Green Slime (page 158)

¾ cup/187.5 g tomato salsa

½ cup/112 g sour cream

2 cups/110 g finely shredded iceberg lettuce

2 cups/180 g shredded Monterey Jack cheese

♥ Slice chicken breasts in half horizontally. Combine lime juice, olive oil, garlic, salt and chili powder and pour into a large zipper-lock bag. Add the chicken, and let marinate for about an hour. Remove the chicken from the marinade to paper towels and pat off most of the marinade.

♥ Heat a cast iron frying pan or grill pan on high heat for 1 to 2 minutes. Add 1 tablespoon/15 ml of canola oil to the pan. As soon as oil begins to smoke, lay the chicken breast pieces in the pan. Let the chicken cook untouched for 2 to 3 minutes, until you have a good sear, then turn the pieces over and cook for another 2 to 3 minutes. After searing the second side, remove chicken and set aside.

♥ Reheat pan on high and add remaining 1 tablespoon/15 ml of oil. As soon as the oil is hot, add the onions and peppers to the pan. Scrape up some of the browned bits from the chicken and stir to coat the onions and peppers. Let them cook undisturbed for 2 minutes. Stir the vegetables and continue to cook for another 2 minutes. Season with salt and pepper. Remove from heat and set aside next to chicken.

♥ Slice the chicken against the grain into strips. Take a tortilla and spread with 2 tablespoons/30 ml Red Spread, leaving borders bare. Dollop 1 tablespoon/15 ml of Green Slime over Red Spread. Place a few table-spoons each of onions, peppers and sliced chicken on lower third of tortilla. Roll bottom edge of tortilla up and around ingredients, grasp tightly and then roll up into a snug roll. Cut on the diagonal. Repeat with remaining ingredients.

♥ Serve with a bunch of sidekicks, like Crunchy Pebbles (page 150), Alligator Scales (page 143), Zucchini Chips (page 146) and Bunny Nibbles (page 149).

FELIX THE CATA-DILLAS
VEGGIE AND CHEESE QUESADILLAS WITH GREEN SLIME

Everybody loves quesadillas, but hardly anyone would imagine how much health can be hidden here in these buttery slices—no fewer than five veggies hide under these calcium-rich, double-cheese quesadillas that are as sly as Felix himself. Serve them with avocado-rich Green Slime and fresh tomato salsa to pack in at least seven vegetables in each bite!

MAKES 2 QUESADILLAS

1 cup/90 g shredded, sharp cheddar cheese

1 cup/90 g shredded Monterey Jack cheese

4 6"/15 cm gluten-free tortillas (page 63)

½ cup/75 g shredded zucchini

⅓ cup/50 g chopped, fresh broccoli

1 red bell pepper, finely chopped

1 carrot, coarsely shredded

4 scallions, finely chopped

2 tablespoons/30 g butter

¾ cup/180 ml Green Slime (page 158)

♥ Mix the two cheeses in a bowl and set aside. Lay 2 tortillas on a workspace. Sprinkle half the cheese evenly over both tortillas. Sprinkle even amounts of veggies over cheese on both tortillas. Sprinkle the remainder of the cheese over the veggies on both tortillas. Top with remaining 2 tortillas. Now your two quesadillas are ready to get melted.

♥ In a large skillet, heat the butter over medium heat until melted, and place one quesadilla in the butter. Set a smaller skillet on top and let quesadilla cook for about 4 minutes. Flip over and repeat on the other side. Remove to cutting board while you repeat the same process for other quesadilla. Cut quesadillas into quarters and serve immediately, or let cool and wrap in parchment paper, then plastic wrap and refrigerate or freeze.

♥ Serve with Green Slime, corn chips and your favorite salsa. Loyal sidekicks are Bunny Nibbles (page 149) and Scooby Doos (page 131).

PIZZA-TILLAS
TORTILLAS WITH MOZZARELLA, CHICKEN AND ROASTED PEPPERS

This recipe calls for Quick Tomato Sauce, but if you are pressed for time, use your favorite prepared tomato sauce—though fresh tomatoes edge out the canned competition with more vitamins A and C, and one tomato providing almost 40% of your daily requirements. A swipe of Red Spread adds more nutrition from sweet peppers. You can also substitute Schmoo for a more herbal taste.

MAKES 2 LARGE TORTILLAS

2 10"-12"/25-30 cm gluten-free tortillas (page 63)

½ cup/120 ml Red Spread (page 156)

1 cup/240 ml Quick Tomato Sauce (page 167)

2 cups/110 g roughly chopped, baby spinach

1 cup/112 g shredded, organic mozzarella or cheddar cheese

1 cup/140 g finely shredded, cooked chicken

½ cup/70 g roughly chopped, roasted red bell peppers

♥ Preheat oven to 450°F/232°C.

♥ Place tortillas on a baking sheet and spread a thin layer of Red Spread over surface, leaving a 1-inch/2.5 cm border all around the edges.

♥ Spread a thin layer of tomato sauce over spread. Top with an even layer of spinach. Add a light layer of shredded chicken followed by a sprinkling of roasted bell peppers. Cover all with a light blanket of cheese.

♥ Place baking sheet in oven and bake for 5 to 10 minutes, until cheese is melted.

♥ Remove from oven and slide onto a cutting board. While still warm but not too hot to touch, firmly roll the tortillas up and rest them on their seams for 5 minutes before slicing into even pieces or in half diagonally.

"YUMMY—I LIKE THE DOUGH AND THE FILLING. YOU COULD CALL IT 'CRAZY PIZZA.'" —CHARLES, AGE 8

GLUTEN-FREE TORTILLAS

Make a double batch of these delicious tortillas so you can freeze half. After cooking, stack tortillas with parchment or waxed paper between each one, wrap the stack in plastic wrap and store in a large zipper-lock freezer bag until ready to use. Let them thaw in the refrigerator overnight or defrost in the microwave.

MAKES ABOUT 10 TORTILLAS

2½ cups/275 g gluten-free, all-purpose flour mix

½ cup/60 g gluten-free, buckwheat flour

2 teaspoons/5 g xanthan gum

1 teaspoon/4.6 g gluten-free baking powder

2 teaspoons/7.5 g brown sugar

½ teaspoon garlic powder

1 teaspoon/6.7 g salt

3 tablespoons/45 ml olive oil

1 tablespoon/15 ml honey

¼ teaspoon apple cider vinegar

2 eggs whisked with ¼ cup/60 ml hot water

1½ cups/360 ml hot water

½ cup /120 ml soy or almond milk

♥ In a large bowl, stir together the all-purpose flour mix, buckwheat flour, xanthan gum, baking powder, brown sugar, garlic powder and salt; set aside.

♥ In a medium bowl, combine the olive oil, honey, vinegar, egg mixture, hot water and soy milk. Pour the wet ingredients into the dry and mix until the batter is smooth, about 1 minute (it will look very gloppy at first).

♥ Heat a lightly oiled griddle pan over medium-high heat. It's hot enough when a drop of water sizzles and bounces across the surface. With a large spoon ready in one hand and an ice cream scoop in the other, scoop a portion of batter onto the hot pan and immediately use the back of the spoon to spread the batter out to a thin 6-inch/15 cm disc. Let the tortilla cook for a minute until firm and bubbles form around the edge. Using a thin, large spatula, flip the tortilla and cook for about another minute until done. Place the cooked tortilla on a flat surface to cool, about 3 minutes. Repeat the process to make a total of 10 tortillas.

CHAPTER THREE

ROLLS

This novel approach in the kitchen will have you and your kids rolling like pros in no time. Let's face it, rolls are more fun than the old square sandwich and they stealthily hold a remarkable amount of wholesome fillings. **This chapter and some others that follow use some specialty wraps you need to order online. They are great, gluten-free, and packed with nutrients, and kids love them.**

Origami wraps can be used in place of seaweed wraps, and Gem Wraps can replace tortillas, bread or lavish. Either can be ordered at newgemfoods.com. There are also rice wrappers, which offer the soft texture of regular sandwich bread without the empty carbs and gluten. Savory nori, covertly packed with amino acids and minerals, rounds out the fun for our delicious wrappers. So, shall we? Let's roll!

ORIGAMI ROLLS
MINI ROLLS WITH SESAME LEMON RICE

Rolling your own sushi rolls is easy with Origami Wraps and a sushi mat. Just a little bit of rice goes a long way—less is best! Make sure your lemon zest is very finely grated and well mixed, and leave out the sesame seeds if your younger eaters are suspicious of brown bits in their rice. To save time, prep carrots and cucumbers the night before. You can also prepare Easy and Perfect Sushi Rice the night before and reheat in microwave before rolling. Feel free to use traditional nori sheets as Origami substitutes.

MAKES ABOUT 6 MINI ROLLS

¼ teaspoon finely grated lemon zest

3 teaspoons/14.3 g sesame seeds, toasted (optional)

1 teaspoon/5.7 g crystal salt flakes

2 cups/420 g Easy and Perfect Sushi Rice (page 128)

1 half-sheet each Origami Corn, Carrot and Tomato Wraps

½ hothouse cucumber, seeded and cut into ¼" X 4"/0.6 x 10 cm strips

½ cup/55 g peeled and shredded carrot

♥ Combine the zest, sesame seeds, and salt (if using) and gently fold the mixture into warm Easy and Perfect Sushi Rice. Set aside.

♥ Peel plastic backing off Origami Corn Wrap and place it (or half sheet nori), shiny side down, on a sushi rolling mat. Allow a ½"/1.3 cm space between bottom of mat and bottom edge of wrap.

♥ Wet hands and press ⅓ cup/70 g Sushi Rice evenly in a thin layer across the wrap, leaving a ¾-inch/1.9-cm rice-free border at the top. Lay two pairs of cucumber strips across lower third of rice, protruding slightly over the end of the wrappers but with no overlapping in the middle.

♥ Lightly swipe top border with a wet, but not dripping, brush. Be careful to evenly dampen the whole border.

♥ Roll forward using mat, and let roll rest on seam for at least 1 minute to seal.

♥ Repeat with Carrot and Tomato Origami Wraps, alternating cucumber strips and shredded carrot as filling.

♥ Serve whole with tamari or teriyaki sauce for dipping.

• •

One Carrot Origami Wrap has the antioxidant value of 5 baby carrots.

PIRATES' BOOTY ROLL
SALTED CHICKEN THIGHS WITH RED BELL PEPPER ORIGAMI WRAPS

Seasoned only with salt and a little black pepper, this chicken is a great and easy alternative to fried chicken. It is fine to substitute a tortilla for this roll.

MAKES 4 ROLLS

4 skin-on, chicken thighs, excess fat trimmed

Kosher salt

Freshly ground black pepper

1 teaspoon/2.5 g cornstarch

1 tablespoon/15 ml canola oil

4 Red Bell Pepper Origami Wraps

1 cup/210 g Easy and Perfect Sushi Rice (page 128)

2 tablespoons/30 ml Red Spread (page 156)

♥ Sprinkle salt over the chicken thoroughly on both sides, rubbing it well onto skin. Place in a large plastic storage bag and let marinate in the refrigerator for at least an hour or overnight.

♥ Preheat oven to 450°F/232°C.

♥ Dry off thighs well with paper towels. Sprinkle both sides lightly with fresh pepper. Rub cornstarch only on the skin to make them extra crispy!

♥ Heat oil in an 8-10"/20-25 cm heavy-bottomed skillet (cast iron is best) on high until very hot but not smoking. Add chicken thighs, skin side down. Fry chicken for about 3 minutes. Reduce heat to medium-high and continue cooking skin-side down about 10 minutes more. Jostle the chicken thighs occasionally to cook evenly and prevent skin from sticking. Leaving skin-side down, transfer to oven for another 15 minutes.

♥ Let chicken thighs rest 10 minutes before pulling the meat off the bone. Cut the meat into ½"/1.3 cm slices crosswise. Use immediately or refrigerate in an airtight container for up to 5 days.

♥ Peel plastic backing off one Origami Red Bell Pepper Wrap and place, shiny side down, on sushi rolling mat. Allow a ½"/1.3 cm space between bottom of mat and bottom edge of wrap.

♥ Wet hands and press ¼ cup/ 52 g Sushi Rice evenly in a thin layer across the wrap, leaving a ¾-inch/1.9-cm rice-free border at the top. Swipe one quarter of the Red Spread in a thin line across lower third of rice, and lay one quarter of the chicken strips over Red Spread.

♥ Lightly swipe top border with a wet, but not dripping, brush. Dampen the whole border evenly. Roll forward using mat and let roll rest on its seam for at least 1 minute to seal. Repeat with remaining ingredients.

♥ Serve with Orange Tamari Sauce (page 166) or a sweet Thai chili sauce.

♥ Serve Hearts and Stars (page 134) and Bunny Nibbles (page 149) as sidekicks.

CHICKEN RUN WRAP
SWEET AND SOUR CHICKEN IN ORIGAMI WRAPS

The taste-bud party that sweet n' sour chicken hosts is a favorite of kids all over the world. When testing recipes, from Hong Kong to New Jersey, I found this wrap always scored highest. This chicken tastes best if you can marinate it overnight—but even an hour will let the flavor shine through. It tastes great rolled with a tortilla as a burrito, too.

MAKES 4 ROLLS

2 pounds/900 g boneless, skinless chicken thighs, cut into bite-sized pieces (white meat is also fine)

1 tablespoon/15 ml tamari sauce

2 tablespoons/15 g fresh ginger, chopped

1 clove garlic, pressed

¼ cup/60 ml water

4 cups/946 ml canola oil, for frying

2 cups/300 g rice crumbs

4 Origami Red Bell Pepper or Carrot Ginger Wraps

½ red bell pepper, cut into 4" x ¼"/10 x 0.6 cm strips (optional)

3 cups/630 g Easy and Perfect Sushi Rice (page 128)

sweet Thai chili sauce for dipping

- In a large zipper-lock bag, mix the chicken, tamari sauce, ginger, garlic and water. Marinate in the refrigerator overnight or for at least 1 hour.

- In a medium frying pan, heat oil over medium heat to 350°F/177°C.

- Place the rice crumbs in another zipper-lock bag. Working with four or five pieces of chicken at a time, take them out of the marinade and add them to the rice crumbs and toss to coat.

- Fry coated chicken in batches for about 2 minutes until golden brown. Use a slotted spoon to transfer chicken to a cooling rack while you finish the rest of the chicken pieces. When all the chicken is finished, cut into ¼"/0.6 cm slices and set aside to roll.

- Peel plastic backing off one Origami Wrap and place, shiny side down, on rolling mat. Leave a ½"/1.3 cm space between bottom of mat and bottom edge of wrap.

- Wet hands and press ¾ cup/160 g Sushi Rice evenly in a thin layer across the wrap, leaving a ¾-inch/1.9-cm rice-free border at the top. Place 3 to 4 pepper strips (if using) followed by 5 to 6 chicken strips in an even line across lower third of rice, protruding slightly over the end of the wrapper.

- Lightly swipe the top border with a wet, but not dripping, brush. Be careful to evenly dampen the whole border.

- Roll forward using mat and let roll rest on its seam for at least 1 minute to seal. Repeat with remaining ingredients. Serve with the sweet Thai chili sauce.

- Sidekicks can be Hearts and Stars (page 134) and Bunny Nibbles (page 149).

MERMAID ROLLS
SALMON SUSHI ROLLS WITH LEMON RICE

I was happy to learn from my recipe-testing sessions that most kids enjoyed smoked salmon. They might not know salmon is an omega-3/vitamin D dynamo that helps their cognitive function, but they knew they loved the salmon with zesty lemon rice and a cool cucumber crunch. This roll is a nobler alternative to bologna and cheese and is delicious with a nori or Origami Red Bell Pepper Wrap.

MAKES 4 ROLLS

4 ounces/113 g smoked salmon, roughly chopped (Nova or Danish smoked salmon is usually less salty and a tad sweeter than lox)

4 tablespoons/60 ml of Red Spread (page 156)

4 half-sheets nori

2 cups/420 g Easy and Perfect Sushi Rice (page 128)

½ English cucumber, seeded and cut into ¼" x 4"/0.6 x 10 cm strips

♥ Combine smoked salmon with Red Spread.

♥ Cover your sushi rolling mat with plastic wrap. Lay one half sheet nori, shiny side down, on rolling mat. Leave a ½"/1.3 cm space between bottom of mat and bottom edge of wrap.

♥ Wet hands and press ⅓ cup/70 g Sushi Rice evenly in a thin layer across the nori, leaving a ¾-inch/1.8-cm rice-free border at the top. Pat about 4 to 5 teaspoons/20 g of salmon mixture across lower third of rice. Place 2 sticks of cucumber across salmon mixture.

♥ Roll forward using mat and let roll rest on seam for at least 1 minute to seal. (No need to swipe border of nori with water.) Repeat with remaining ingredients.

♥ Serve with Orange Tamari Sauce (page 166) for dipping. For sidekicks, try Sweeties (page 139) and Hearts and Stars (page 134).

PUSS N' BOOTS
CALIFORNIA TUNA SALAD ROLLS WITH ORIGAMI TOMATO WRAPS

Tuna fish provides omega-3s, which support eyes, hearts and hormones-meow! And three raw veggies hide their acid-balancing act in Schmoo's or Red Spread's creamy deliciousness. This powerhouse roll is a sneaky knockout of healthy delight.

MAKES 2 ROLLS

1 6-oz/168-g can light tuna, packed in water, drained

1 tablespoon/15 g mayonnaise

1 teaspoon/5 ml fresh lemon juice

2 Origami Tomato Wraps

1 cup (210 g) Easy and Perfect Sushi Rice (page 128)

4 tablespoons/60 ml Schmoo (page 161) or Red Spread (page 156)

½ English or hothouse cucumber, seeded and cut into ¼" x 4"/0.6 x 10 cm strips

1 medium carrot, coarsely shredded

½ avocado, pitted, skinned and sliced ¼"/0.6 cm-thick lengthwise

♥ Put drained tuna fish in the middle of 2 paper towels and twist up into a ball to squeeze out extra water to get the tuna as dry as possible. In a small bowl, mix tuna fish, mayonnaise and lemon juice and mix well. (You can make this the night before, along with prepping the cucumbers and carrots.)

♥ Peel plastic backing off one Origami Wrap and place, shiny side down, on rolling mat. Leave a ½"/1.3 cm space between bottom of mat and bottom edge of wrap.

♥ Wet hands and press ½ cup/105 g Sushi Rice evenly in a thin layer across the wrap, leaving a ¾-inch/1.9-cm rice-free border at the top. Spread 2 tablespoons/30 ml of Schmoo or Red Spread across lower third of rice. Press 1 to 2 tablespoons/13.8 g of carrot into the spread, 2 tablespoons/13 g cucumber, then 2 tablespoons/28 g tuna mixture, followed by 3 to 4 strips of avocado.

♥ Lightly swipe the top border with a wet, but not dripping, brush. Be careful to evenly dampen the whole border. Roll forward using mat and let roll rest on its seam for at least 1 minute to seal. Cut crosswise into 8 even pieces. Repeat with remaining ingredients.

♥ Serve with Sharky Chips (page 145) and Bark Bites (page 136) for dessert.

"IT'S SO YUMMY! DID A GREEN GODDESS MAKE THIS?" —TOBIA, AGE 4

THE GREEN GODDESS ROLL
GREEN VEGGIES ROLL WITH AVOCADO, ASPARAGUS AND SCALLION

Let's count the RAW ways your kid will roll with The Goddess. Avocado, cucumber, scallion, parsley, spinach, basil, garlic and lemon juice, not to mention the super-food nori, which has more Vitamin C per serving than an orange. Whew! That's a Super-Stealth Hefty-Health Roll with a magical name.

MAKES 4 ROLLS

8 stalks thin asparagus, trimmed to 4"/10 cm

2 teaspoons/10 ml olive oil

Salt and pepper, to taste

4 half-sheets nori

2 cups/420 g Easy and Perfect Sushi Rice (page 128)

1 tablespoon/15 ml toasted sesame seeds (optional)

3 scallions, finely chopped (optional)

1 avocado, peeled, pitted and cut lengthwise into ¼"/0.6 cm strips

1 hothouse or English cucumber, seeded and cut into ¼" x 4"/0.6 x 10 cm strips

½ cup/120 ml Orange Tamari Sauce (page 166)

½ cup/120 ml Green Goddess Dressing (page 163)

♥ Heat a grill pan over medium-high heat. Lightly toss asparagus with olive oil, and season with salt and pepper. Grill asparagus for about 3 minutes, or until bright green and still crisp.

♥ Cover your sushi rolling mat with plastic wrap. Place one half-sheet nori on the rolling mat. Wet hands and spread about ½ cup/105 g of Easy and Perfect Sushi Rice evenly over entire nori. Sprinkle surface of rice with sesame seeds, if using. Flip the nori sheet over and arrange on mat, allowing a ½-inch/1.3-cm border between bottom edge of mat and long bottom edge of nori.

♥ Scatter a teaspoon of scallions across the middle of the nori. Arrange two pairs of asparagus spears end-to-end (heads out) on top of scallions. Arrange 3 to 4 strips of the avocado alongside the asparagus. Lay 2 pairs of cucumber strips on top of avocado. Roll forward using mat and let roll rest on its seam for at least 1 minute to seal. Cut crosswise into 8 even pieces. Repeat with remaining ingredients.

♥ Serve with Orange Tamari Sauce and Green Goddess Dressing for dipping.

CATERPILLAR ROLL
CUCUMBER AND AVOCADO INSIDE-OUT NORI ROLLS

This darling bug of a roll wears a sly coat of avocado—one of the healthiest fruits on the planet. Your little chef will be excited about making antennae and eyes for this healthy roll!

MAKES 2 CATERPILLARS

½ medium carrot, peeled and halved crosswise

1 avocado, pitted and split lengthwise

1 ½ cups/315 g Easy and Perfect Sushi Rice (page 128)

2 half-sheets nori

½ English cucumber, cut into 4" x ¼"/10 x 0.6 cm sticks

2 teaspoons/9.5 g sesame seeds (optional garnish)

½ cup/120 ml Orange Tamari Sauce (page 166)

♥ Chop the skinny end of the carrot into 10 to 12 small, thin discs. These are the eyes and spots of your bug. Now cut carrot in half lengthwise. Lay flat side down and trim off 4 long, slender strips that get thinner at one end. These will be the antennae. Set aside.

♥ Scoop out the avocado flesh with a tablespoon, keeping it in one whole piece. Set it hole-side down and cut crosswise into very thin slices. (Avocado is easiest to slice by putting your knife tip 2"/5 cm above the avocado half and pulling the knife through the flesh.)

♥ Cover your sushi rolling mat with plastic wrap. Place one nori sheet on the rolling mat. Wet hands and spread about ½ cup/105 g of Easy and Perfect Sushi Rice evenly over entire nori. Flip the nori sheet over and arrange on mat, allowing a ½"/1.3 cm border between bottom edge of mat and long bottom edge of nori. Place two double sticks of cucumber in a line across the middle of the nori. Roll forward using mat, let roll rest on its seam for at least 1 minute to seal. Repeat for remaining roll.

♥ Now, slide a long knife under one sliced avocado half and place it on top of the sushi roll and fan it out (like dominoes) to fit end to end. Take a sheet of plastic wrap and cover the roll. Place the sushi mat over the roll and give it a gentle squeeze to adhere the avocado to the rice.

♥ Remove mat and, leaving plastic wrap in place, cut through plastic into 8 even pieces. Use a very sharp knife for this or it will squish the bug. Gently pull off the plastic wrap. Now the little chefs can come decorate.

♥ Place carrot eyes and line spots down the back. Stick in two antennae near the head. Sprinkle on sesame seeds if desired. Repeat with remaining roll.

♥ Serve with Orange Tamari Sauce for dipping and Crunchy Pebbles (page 150), Origami Crisps (page 140) or Bunny Nibbles (page 149) as sidekicks.

FLOWER POWER SUSHI
CUCUMBER AND PICKLED CARROT INSIDE-OUT NORI ROLLS

These little petals take more rolling than other rolls, but they are so worth the extra effort. They are almost too pretty to eat—almost. And they are great with all kinds of dipping sauces.

MAKES 4 ROLLS

1 carrot, cut into 4" x ¼"/10 x 0.6 cm sticks

½ cup/120 ml seasoned rice vinegar

½ English cucumber, cut into 4" x ¼"/10 x 0.6 cm sticks

5 cups/1050 g Easy and Perfect Sushi Rice (page 128)

8 half-sheets nori

4 whole sheets nori

¼ cup/57 g toasted sesame seeds (optional)

Green Dream (page 159), Orange Zinger (page 157) or Orange Tamari Sauce (page 166) for dipping

♥ In a small glass bowl, combine carrot sticks with seasoned rice vinegar and let pickle for about 30 minutes.

♥ Take the 8 half-sheets of nori and cut them in half again, lengthwise. You will have 16 quarter-nori strips. With wet hands, pat a thin, even layer of rice on all strips, leaving a ⅛-inch/0.3-cm border on the long upper edge. Without the mat, roll up each strip to close.

♥ Cover your sushi rolling mat with plastic wrap. Place one whole nori sheet, shiny side down, on the rolling mat. Wet hands and spread about ¾ to 1 cup/160 to 210 g of Easy and Perfect Sushi Rice evenly over entire nori. Sprinkle the surface evenly with 2 tablespoons/28 g sesame seeds, if using. Flip the nori sheet over and arrange on mat allowing a ½-inch/1.3-cm border between bottom edge of mat and long, bottom edge of nori. Now press another ¾ cup/160 g rice evenly across the nori, leaving a 1-inch/2.5-cm border at the top.

♥ Lay 2 sticks of cucumber in a line across middle of the rice. Place 2 mini sushi rolls on either side of cucumber with a ⅛-inch/0.3-cm space between each. Fill in slots between mini rolls with 2 strips of carrots. Now you have, from bottom to top: a mini roll, a carrot line, another mini roll, a cucumber line, a mini roll, a carrot line and a final mini roll.

♥ Roll forward using mat and let roll rest on its seam for at least 1 minute to seal.

♥ Repeat to form remaining 3 rolls. Cut each roll crosswise into 8 even pieces.

♥ Serve with Origami Crisps (page 140), Bunny Nibbles (page 149) or Crunchy Pebbles (page 150).

. . . .

If your little ones don't like pickled carrots, these rolls are good with plain carrots too. Just omit the first step.

SHRIMP SWEETIES

COCONUT SHRIMP AND MANGO IN ORIGAMI MANGO WRAPS

This lovely pairing of fruity mango and crunchy coconut shrimp is delicious. Luscious mangoes are good for eyesight and digestion, while crunchy coconut is fun to eat and is full of good antioxidants to boost immune systems. This recipe works well with chicken strips in place of shrimp. Just cook chicken strips about twice as long at 375°F/191°C. This is tasty with traditional nori as well.

MAKES 4 ROLLS

Juice of 1 lime

1 mango, peeled, halved, seeded and cut into ¼"x 4"/0.6 x 10 cm sticks

¼ cup/60 ml honey

½ pound/230 g fresh or frozen large shrimp, peeled and deveined

Salt, to taste

½ cup/113.4 g unsweetened, flaked coconut

½ cup/75 g rice crumbs

2 ½ cups/525 g Easy and Perfect Sushi Rice (page 128)

½ English cucumber, seeded and cut into ¼" x 4"/0.6 x 10 cm sticks

4 Origami Mango Wraps

▾ Preheat oven to 425°F/218°C.

▾ In a blender, combine lime juice, 1 cup/150 g of the chopped mangoes and the honey; cover and process until smooth. Place ¼ cup/60 ml of the mango mixture in a shallow dish and set aside. Transfer remaining mixture to a small serving bowl and set aside to use as dipping sauce.

▾ Rinse shrimp and pat dry with paper towels. Sprinkle shrimp with salt.

▾ Mix coconut and rice crumbs in a shallow dish and place next to mango sauce. Dip shrimp in mango sauce and then in coconut, pressing to coat. Place on an oiled baking rack over a baking sheet.

▾ Bake for 7 to 8 minutes, being careful not to overcook. The high heat will cook the shrimp thoroughly and give the coconut a golden crunch.

▾ Roughly chop the cooked shrimp and set in a small bowl. Include any crunchy bits from chopping board.

▾ Peel plastic backing off one Origami Wrap and place, shiny side down, on work surface. Wet hands, then press a scant ¾ cup/160 g of Sushi Rice over Origami Wrap in an even layer (about 3 to 4 grains thick), leaving a 2-inch/5-cm bare border at the top. Place one quarter of the cucumber sticks in an even line across lower third of rice.

▾ Scatter about 3 to 4 tablespoons/28 g of chopped shrimp over cucumbers. Lightly swipe the top border of the wrap with a wet, but not dripping, brush. Be careful to evenly dampen the whole border. Roll forward using mat and let roll rest on its seam for at least 1 minute to seal. Repeat with remaining ingredients. Cut crosswise into 8 even pieces and serve with remaining mango sauce or Orange Tamari Sauce (page 166) and Sharky Chips (page 145).

CHAPTER FOUR

GEM WRAPS

This chapter is all about my Gem Wraps. These all-natural, gluten-free, vegetable and fruit wraps are low-carb, low calorie, and artificial ingredient-free to use as alternatives to tortillas, bread and lavash. And the unique flavors allow you to create new versions of old favorites with a fraction of the sodium. Behind their glossy, colorful, show-girl surfaces, these wraps are nutritional workhorses packed with hidden antioxidants and vitamins. **As mentioned in the previous chapter, some of the recipes here require specialty wraps you order online at newgemfoods.com.**

PINWHEELS
TURKEY AND CHEESE ROLL-UPS

These colorful pinwheels put a real spin on the usual turkey and cheese sandwiches. Packed with the hidden veggie power of sweet bell peppers or fresh herbs and spinach in the cream spread of your choice, your little ones will never know they are filling up on so many super-healthy ingredients with these yummy whirlygigs.

MAKES 2 PINWHEELS

2 Carrot Gem Wraps

2 tablespoons/30 ml Red Spread (page 156) or Schmoo (page 161)

2 lightly packed handfuls rinsed baby spinach leaves, chopped

2 Roma tomatoes, cut crosswise into thin slices

4 slices Swiss or cheddar cheese

4 thin slices turkey breast

♥ Peel plastic backing off of one Carrot Gem Wrap and lay, shiny side down, on a work surface.

♥ Spread 1 tablespoon/15 ml of the spread of your choice all over wrap except for a 2-inch/5-cm border at the top. Sprinkle with spinach and top with tomato slices. Arrange 2 slices Swiss cheese and 2 slices turkey in even layers over the vegetables.

♥ Dip a brush into a bowl of cool water, then dab brush onto a towel and swipe the top border of the Gem Wrap, making sure you get it evenly moistened. Then fold bottom edge of Wrap up and around ingredients and roll tightly forward. Let rest on the seam for a minute or two before cutting on the diagonal or crosswise into 8 even pieces. Repeat with remaining ingredients.

♥ Serve with Bunny Nibbles (page 149), Zucchini Chips (page 146) and Grecian Dip (page 160) and/or Crunchy Pebbles (page 150).

HONEY BEARS AND BANANA BITES

OATMEAL-PEACH AND PEANUT BUTTER—BANANA ROLL-UPS

Just 1 cup of oatmeal has 10 grams of protein and is great soluble fiber. Honey is a natural energy booster and each Mango Gem Wrap is equivalent to about 2 whole mangoes, making this a perfect after-school snack or breakfast for your healthy kid. Swap halved strawberries for peaches if peaches are not available.

MAKES 2 WRAPS

FOR HONEY BEARS

2 Mango Gem Wraps

1½ cups/350 g prepared, instant Irish Oatmeal, cooled

1 medium, fresh peach, peeled, sliced thin and cut into 4" X ¼"/10 X 0.6 cm sticks

2 ounces/56 g raisins, dried sweetened cranberries, apricots or dates

1 teaspoon/5 ml orange juice

¼ cup/60 ml honey for drizzling or dipping sauce

½ cup/45 g granola

FOR BANANA BITES

2 Mango Gem Wraps

1 cup/260 g smooth peanut butter

½ cup/45 g granola

2 bananas

¼ cup/60 ml honey

FOR EACH HONEY BEAR:

♥ Peel plastic backing off Gem Wrap and place, shiny side down, on work surface.

♥ Wet hands and dab partly dry, then pat half of the oatmeal over Gem Wrap in an even layer, leaving a 2-inch/5-cm bare border at the top. Sprinkle half the raisins over the oatmeal and press in a little to secure. Place a single line of peaches across lower third of oatmeal.

♥ Dip a brush into a bowl of cool water, then dab onto a towel. Swipe the top border of the Gem Wrap, making sure you get it evenly moistened. Then fold bottom edge of Wrap up and around ingredients and roll tightly forward. Let rest on the seam for a minute or two before cutting on the diagonal. Cut into 8 pieces.

♥ Mix the orange juice with the honey. Drizzle each piece with a little honey and granola, and use remaining honey as a dipping sauce.

FOR EACH BANANA BITE:

♥ Peel plastic backing off Gem Wrap and place, shiny side down, on work surface.

♥ With a rubber spatula, swipe half of the peanut butter over wrap, leaving 2-inch/5-cm borders at top and bottom of wrap. Sprinkle granola across peanut butter and press in gently. Place banana horizontally across middle of peanut butter/granola.

♥ Dip a brush into a bowl of cool water, then dab onto a towel. Swipe the top border of the Gem Wrap, making sure you get it evenly moistened. Then fold bottom edge of Wrap up and around ingredients and roll tightly forward. Let rest on the seam for a minute before cutting on the diagonal.

ORANGE CHICKEN CRUNCH WRAPS
CHICKEN SALAD WITH ORANGES AND CHINESE NOODLES

Use any leftover chicken for this Asian twist on the classic chicken salad. This chicken boasts a silky sesame coating mixed with sparkling orange segments and crunchy peanuts or Crispy Rice Noodles. Wrapped in a bright orange coat, this wrap pleases eyes and mouth while providing the vitamin C punch of fresh orange and the pure protein of chicken.

MAKES 4 CARROT GEM WRAPS

2 tablespoons/28 g mayonnaise

1½ teaspoons/7.5 ml sesame oil

2 cups/280 g shredded, cooked chicken

1 small celery rib, finely diced

½ cup/60 g fresh orange segments, chopped

¼ cup/40 g coarsely chopped, roasted, unsalted peanuts (optional)

¼ cup/19 g Crispy Rice Noodles (page 135) (optional)

4 Carrot Gem Wraps

4 leaves green leaf or iceberg lettuce, finely shredded

♥ Whisk together the mayonnaise and sesame oil. Combine the mayonnaise mixture, chicken and celery in a bowl and mix. Gently fold in orange segments and peanuts or Crispy Rice Noodles, if using.

♥ Peel plastic backing off one Gem Wrap and place, shiny side down, on work surface. Scatter one quarter of the shredded lettuce across lower third of Gem Wrap, leaving a 2-inch/5 cm border at the top. Spread about ½ cup/62.5 g of chicken salad mixture evenly over lettuce. Swipe top border with a wet (but not dripping) brush and roll tightly to close. Repeat with remaining ingredients. Serve with extra orange segments.

HOT WINGS WRAPS
SPICY CHICKEN WITH BLUE CHEESE SLAW

Cabbage with a K! Vitamin K, that is. Vitamin K is good for bones, and cabbage provides lots of fiber. Hot pepper sauce is packed with vitamin A, and who won't love tender chicken swathed in creamy cool coleslaw with a hint of blue cheese? All wrapped up in an easy Carrot Gem Wrap, it's like adding a whole extra carrot to your roll. Get extra chicken tenders for dinner and set aside a portion for your Hot Wings. You can also assemble the coleslaw the night before and dress right before rolling.

MAKES 4 WRAPS

3 cups/630 g Easy and Perfect Sushi Rice (page 128)

1 pound/450 g chicken tenders

1½ cups/180 g coleslaw mix, finely shredded

1 celery stalk, thinly sliced

2 tablespoons/30 ml blue cheese dressing (or ranch, if preferred), plus more for dipping

1 cup/240 ml hot pepper sauce (such as Frank's), divided

4 tablespoons/56.7 g unsalted butter

4 Carrot Gem Wraps

♥ In a zipper-lock bag, soak chicken tenders in 1 cup/240 ml room-temperature water for 30 minutes.

♥ In the meantime, mix coleslaw mix and celery and toss with the blue cheese dressing.

♥ In a large skillet, melt butter and ¼ cup/60 ml hot sauce and whisk to blend. On medium-low heat, add chicken tenders to sauce and cook until cooked through, about 5 to 7 minutes. Remove to a cutting board and cut lengthwise into 4 x ¼-inch/10 x 0.6-cm strips.

♥ Peel plastic backing off Gem Wrap and place, shiny side down, on work surface. Press ½ cup/105 g Sushi Rice over Wrap, leaving a 2-inch/5-cm border bare at the top. Spread 3 to 4 tablespoons/23 to 30 g of coleslaw across lower third of rice. Scatter about ½ cup/75 g chicken over slaw.

♥ Dip a brush into a bowl of cool water, then dab brush onto a towel. Swipe the top border of the Gem Wrap, making sure you get it evenly moistened. Then fold bottom edge of Wrap up and around ingredients and roll tightly forward. Let rest on the seam for a minute or two before cutting on the diagonal. Repeat with remaining ingredients. Serve with extra blue cheese dressing for dipping.

MARIO WRAPS
CHICKEN PARMESAN ROLL

Everybody's favorite Italian brother, Mario, created this roll from his favorite ingredients: Italian sausage, mozzarella and tomatoes. Mangia with Mario and get the antioxidant lycopene and rich calcium boost it offers.

MAKES 4 BIG WRAPS

1 cup/120 g gluten-free flour

1 teaspoon/6.7 g Kosher salt

½ teaspoon freshly ground black pepper

2 large eggs

1 tablespoon/15 ml water

Pinch of salt

1¼ cups/190 g rice crumbs

½ cup/45 g grated Parmesan cheese

2 boneless, skinless chicken breasts

2 tablespoons/28 g unsalted butter

2 tablespoons/30 ml extra-virgin olive oil

1 cup/240 ml Quick Tomato Sauce (page 167)

1 cup/90 g shredded mozzarella cheese

4 Tomato Gem Wraps

4 cups/120 g roughly chopped spinach

♥ In a large zipper-lock bag, mix together the flour, salt and pepper.

♥ In a shallow dish, beat the eggs with 1 tablespoon/15 ml water and a pinch of salt. In a second shallow dish, combine the rice crumbs and grated Parmesan. Drop the chicken breasts in flour bag and shake to coat. Remove floured chicken breasts and roll in egg mixture, then press into rice crumb mixture to coat.

♥ Preheat oven to 375°F/190°C.

♥ Heat butter and olive oil in a large skillet and cook chicken breasts on medium heat for 3 minutes on each side, until cooked through. Lay the chicken in a baking dish and lightly spoon some Quick Tomato Sauce over it. Sprinkle the mozzarella on top and bake for 5 to 6 minutes, until cheese is melted. Remove chicken from oven and let cool. Place chicken on a cutting board and cut lengthwise into ½-inch/1.3 cm strips.

♥ Peel plastic backing off one Gem Wrap and place, shiny side down, on work surface. Sprinkle ½ cup/15 g spinach across lower third. Place two strips of chicken over spinach. Cover chicken strips with about another ½ cup/15 g spinach. (Enclosing the chicken with spinach will prevent the wrap from getting soggy.)

♥ Dip a brush into a bowl of cool water, then dab brush onto a towel. Swipe the top border of the Gem Wrap, making sure you get it evenly moistened. Then fold bottom edge of wrap up and around ingredients and roll tightly forward. Let rest on the seam for a minute or two before cutting on the diagonal. Repeat with remaining ingredients.

♥ Serve with extra Quick Tomato Sauce for dipping and Zucchini Chips (page 146).

CHICKEN IN A BLANKET

BBQ CHICKEN IN ASSORTED GEM WRAPS

Chicken is the Big Bird of essential nutrients and vitamins, including niacin (vitamin B3), which helps turn carbs into energy. Kids will love this sweet and tangy version of a BBQ sandwich without bread. Tuck some shredded veggies into your Red or Golden Spread to get an extra healthy boost! The chicken can be grilled outside or inside for this recipe. Or, just use leftovers or buy it already prepared from your market.

MAKES 2 WRAPS

2 whole, chicken legs quarters

Salt and freshly ground black pepper, to taste

½ cup/120 ml your favorite barbecue sauce

2 Gem Wraps (Tomato, Carrot, Mango or BBQ)

1 cup/210 g Easy and Perfect Sushi Rice (page 128)

½ cup/120 ml Red Spread (page 156) or Golden Spread (page 162)

¼ cup/25 g finely chopped scallions

½ cup/15 g finely shredded spinach

½ cup/75 g finely shredded carrot

♥ Heat a greased grill (or grill pan) to medium-low. Season both sides of the chicken legs with salt and pepper. Place the chicken on the grill, skin side down, and grill about 15 minutes. Turn legs over and, with a basting brush, brush some barbecue sauce onto the chicken legs. Keep grilling, turning legs occasionally and brushing on barbecue sauce each time for another 15 to 20 minutes. Remove from grill and let cool. Shred chicken meat into a bowl and set aside. Or, just toss leftover chicken with a little barbecue sauce and go from here.

♥ For each wrap, peel plastic backing off Gem Wrap and place, shiny side down, on work surface. Wet and dab hands partly dry, then pat ½ cup/105 g Sushi Rice across wrap, leaving a 2-inch/5-cm border at the top. Smear ¼ cup/60 ml of Red Spread across middle of rice. Sprinkle 2 tablespoons of scallions on the spread, then scatter half of the spinach and the carrot. Place half the chicken over veggies. Then fold bottom edge of wrap up and around ingredients and roll tightly forward. Let rest on the seam for a minute or two before cutting on the diagonal. Repeat with remaining ingredients.

♥ Serve with Hearts and Stars (page 134), Origami Crisps (page 140) or Alligator Scales (page 143).

> "THE BEST SO FAR. LOVE THE CHICKEN; LOVE THE WRAPPER. CALL IT 'CHICKEN BLANKETS.'" —LARA, AGE 6

SAUSAGE SIZZLERS
CHICKEN SAUSAGE WITH SWEET PEPPERS

The sizzling sausage can be chicken, pork or turkey, so you know this recipe is versatile. Calcium-rich mozzarella rides in with vitamin-rich sweet bell peppers. These sizzlers are great for the kids to take to school with the marinara sauce in a side container, or for the party after school is out. Try popping this finished roll into the microwave for 5 seconds to melt your mozzarella. Yuuuum.

MAKES 4 SIZZLERS

4 BBQ Gem Wraps

2 cups/420 g Easy and Perfect Sushi Rice (page 128)

¼ cup/60 ml Schmoo (page 161)

½ cup/45 g shredded fresh mozzarella cheese

½ red bell pepper, cut into ¼"/ 0.6 cm strips

2 large, sweet Italian sausages, grilled and cut lengthwise into ¼"/0.6 cm strips

¾ cup/180 ml prepared marinara sauce for dipping

♥ Peel plastic backing off one Gem Wrap and place, shiny side down, on work surface. Press ½ cup/105 g of Sushi Rice in an even layer across the wrap, leaving a 2-inch/5-cm border at the top. Swipe about 1 tablespoon/15 ml of Schmoo across lower third of rice. Sprinkle mozzarella across the Schmoo, then arrange 3 to 4 strips of red bell pepper and 2 sausage strips over the cheese.

♥ Dip a brush into a bowl of cool water, then dab brush onto a towel. Swipe the bare top border of the Gem Wrap, making sure you get it evenly moistened. Then fold bottom edge of wrap up and around ingredients and roll tightly forward. Let rest on the seam for a minute or two before cutting on the diagonal. Repeat with remaining ingredients. Serve with your favorite marinara sauce as a dipping sauce.

CHICKEN SPICE AND EVERYTHING NICE

CHICKEN GYROS WITH GRECIAN DIP

Kids love these chicken fingers marinated in the best Greek ingredients: lemon juice, olive oil and herbs. The herbs are finely ground so there are no "funny specks". Olive oil improves cognitive function, and garlic knocks out bacterial baddies. Feel free to use leftover chicken, and you can prep and bake all the veggies the night before and make the Grecian Dip ahead of time as well.

MAKES 4 WRAPS

3 cloves garlic, pressed

⅛ teaspoon ground oregano

⅛ teaspoon ground thyme

1 teaspoon/6.7 g Kosher salt

¼ teaspoon fresh black pepper

¼ cup/60 ml fresh lemon juice

6 tablespoons/90 ml extra-virgin olive oil

1½ pounds/680 g boneless, skinless chicken breasts, cut into 1"/2.5 cm strips

1 large baking potato or sweet potato, well scrubbed, cut into ½"/1.3 cm thick wedges

Coarse salt for seasoning

½ red bell pepper, seeded and cut into ¼"/0.6 cm strips

½ orange or yellow bell pepper, cut into ¼"/0.6 cm strips

¼ sweet onion (Walla Walla or Vidalia), thinly sliced (optional)

4 Tomato Gem Wraps

1 cup/240 ml Grecian Dip (page 160)

♥ Preheat oven to 450°F/232°C.

♥ In a medium bowl, whisk together the garlic, oregano, thyme, salt, pepper, lemon juice and olive oil. Evenly divide the marinade between two zipper-lock bags. Add the chicken to one bag, toss to coat, and refrigerate for about 2 hours or overnight.

♥ Add potato wedges (either baking or sweet) to the other zipper-lock bag and toss to coat. Place wedges directly on a baking rack set on top of a baking sheet. (With a rack, the heat can circulate under potatoes so you don't have to turn them over halfway through cooking time. If you don't have a rack, do flip them over halfway through!) Bake for about 30 minutes. Remove from oven and place potato wedges on a plate. Immediately sprinkle with a little coarse salt.

♥ Reduce oven heat to 350°F/177°C. Take marinated chicken out of the bag, letting marinade drip off a bit. Place chicken strips on same rack (no need to clean up in between potatoes and chicken) and place in oven. Bake 12 to 15 minutes, until just cooked through.

♥ For each wrap, peel plastic backing off Gem Wrap and place, shiny side down, on work surface. Lay several bell pepper strips on lower third of wrap. Scatter some onion strings over the peppers, if using. Place chicken strips across peppers and onions. Top with potato wedges.

♥ Dip a brush into a bowl of cool water, then dab brush onto a towel. Swipe the top border of the Gem Wrap, making sure you get it evenly moistened. Then fold bottom edge of wrap up and around ingredients and roll tightly forward. Let rest on the seam for a minute before cutting on the diagonal. Repeat with remaining ingredients. Double wrap in parchment and plastic wrap and put in lunchbox with a side of Grecian Dip and Origami Crisps (page 140) or Zucchini Chips (page 146).

"SPICY, JUICY AND DELICIOUS. EVERYTHING NICE!" —BAILEY, AGE 9

GREEN EGGS AND HAM ROLL
SCRAMBLED EGGS AND SPINACH BREAKFAST BURRITOS

Never mind "Sam I Am;" your child will love these green eggs and ham. This is great for a breakfast-for-lunch burrito, packed with egg protein that is especially good for eyes. And spinach—well, we all know what it does for Popeye! Plus, the Tomato Gem Wrap is the secret equivalent of a fresh tomato. This recipe works without rice as well—just add a little more of everything else. You can also swap out the ham for bacon or turkey sausage.

MAKES 2 BURRITOS

3 large eggs

Salt and pepper, to taste

½ cup/45 g grated cheddar or Monterey Jack cheese

2 teaspoons/10 g butter

2 Tomato Gem Wraps

1 cup/210 g Easy and Perfect Sushi Rice (page 128)

1 cup/15 g roughly chopped, baby spinach leaves

4 thin slices ham

½ cup/120 ml Vampire Sauce (page 165), if desired

♥ In a glass mixing bowl, beat eggs with salt and pepper until they are light yellow. Stir in the cheese.

♥ In a skillet, heat the butter over medium-low heat until foaming, about 2 minutes. Add the egg mixture. Cook, folding over gently, until desired doneness. Slide eggs onto a plate to cool.

♥ For each wrap, peel plastic backing off Gem Wrap and place, shiny side down, on work surface. Wet hands and thinly spread about ½ cup/105 g of Sushi Rice evenly over the wrap, leaving a 2-inch/5-cm border at the top. Arrange a line of spinach leaves across lower third of rice. Spoon about half the eggs over spinach. Arrange 2 ham slices trimmed to drape over eggs.

♥ Dip a brush into a bowl of cool water, then dab brush onto a towel. Swipe the bare top border of the Gem Wrap, making sure you get it evenly moistened. Then fold bottom edge of wrap up and around ingredients and roll tightly forward. Let rest on the seam for a minute or two before cutting on the diagonal. Repeat with remaining ingredients.

♥ Serve with Vampire Sauce and Crunchy Pebbles (page 150).

OPEN SESAME WRAP
SESAME SEED-CRUSTED CHICKEN TENDERS WITH MANGO SLAW

Crunchy sesame seeds give this chicken wrap an extra punch of energy. Delightful with mango and coleslaw in an antioxidant-packed Mango or BBQ Gem Wrap.

MAKES 4 WRAPS

½ cup/120 ml soy sauce

1 tablespoon/15 ml sesame oil

2 pounds/900 g chicken tenders

1 tablespoon/7.5 g gluten-free, all-purpose flour or rice flour

1 tablespoon/7.5 g cornstarch

⅛ teaspoon baking powder

4 egg whites

½ cup/72 g toasted sesame seeds

½ cup/75 g rice crumbs

3 cups/710 ml peanut oil, for frying

4 Mango or BBQ Gem Wraps

2 cups/420 g Easy and Perfect Sushi Rice (page 128)

MANGO SLAW

½ mango, sliced into matchstick strips

3 cups/360 g coleslaw mix, shredded

2 tablespoons/30 ml seasoned rice vinegar

½ cup/120 g mayonnaise

2 teaspoons/10 ml fresh lime juice

Salt and freshly ground pepper

- Combine soy sauce, ¼ cup/60 ml water and sesame oil in a large zipper-lock bag and marinate chicken tenders for 20 to 30 minutes.

- Meanwhile, combine flour, cornstarch and baking powder in another large zipper-lock bag and set aside.

- Pour egg whites into a large bowl. Then combine sesame seeds and rice crumbs in a shallow bowl.

- Remove chicken from marinade. Toss in the bag with the flour mixture and shake well. Then dip floured chicken pieces in egg whites. Roll in rice crumb mixture and set chicken tenders aside.

- Heat peanut oil in a deep fryer or large pot to a temperature of 375°F/191°C.

- Drop in the chicken pieces, a few at a time, and fry until they turn crispy golden, 3 to 4 minutes. Drain on baking rack. When cool, split chicken tenders lengthwise and cut into ½-inch x 4-inch/1.3 x 10-cm strips.

- To make the Mango Slaw: Toss all ingredients together.

- For each wrap, peel plastic backing off Gem Wrap and place, shiny side down, on work surface. Press ½ cup/105 g Sushi Rice evenly across wrap, leaving a 2-inch/5-cm border at the top. Dollop about 2 to 3 tablespoons/ 40 to 50 g of Mango Slaw across lower third of rice. Top slaw with an even line of chicken tenders.

- Dip a brush into a bowl of cool water, then dab brush onto a towel. Swipe the bare top border of the Gem Wrap, making sure you get it evenly moistened. Then fold bottom edge of wrap up and around ingredients and roll tightly forward. Let rest on the seam for a minute or two before cutting on the diagonal. Repeat with remaining ingredients.

- Serve with extra Mango Slaw and Orange Tamari Sauce (page 166).

"I JUST WANT TO STUFF MORE IN MY MOUTH!!" —TOBIA, AGE 4

BLT WRAPS
BACON, LETTUCE AND TOMATO IN ORIGAMI TOMATO WRAPS

Everything's better with bacon—even sushi! And the shiny, delicious Tomato Gem Wraps roll it up with an under-the-radar antioxidant and vitamin value of about 3 fresh tomatoes. Kids will enjoy the pretty red wrapping and yummy taste of crispy bacon, cheddar cheese and slivers of tangy tomato. Prep all ingredients the night before—heck, even roll them all the night before. Wrapped in parchment paper, then plastic or foil, the next day these rolls will come to room temperature nicely in your child's lunch box and be the envy of the lunchroom.

MAKES 1 BIG WRAP

1 Tomato Gem Wrap

¾ cup/160 g Easy and Perfect Sushi Rice (page 128)

2 tablespoons/14 g grated cheddar cheese

4 strips bacon, cooked and roughly chopped

2 thick slices tomato, seeded and chopped medium

½ cup/15 g finely shredded Romaine lettuce

♥ Peel plastic backing off Gem Wrap and place, shiny side down, on work surface. Press sushi rice into Tomato Gem Wrap, leaving a 2-inch/5-cm border at top. Sprinkle cheese across lower third of rice. Press in bacon bits over cheese. Sprinkle chopped tomatoes over bacon. Then scatter a layer of lettuce over tomatoes.

♥ Dip a brush into a bowl of cool water, then dab brush onto a towel. Swipe the top border of the Gem Wrap, making sure you get it evenly moistened. Then fold bottom edge of wrap up and around ingredients and roll tightly forward. Let rest on the seam for a minute or two before cutting into 8 pieces.

♥ Serve with tomato salsa and Crunchy Pebbles (page 150) or Zucchini Chips (page 146).

THE PORKIE ROLL
PORK AND AVOCADO BURRITO

This recipe makes several burritos that are fun for kids to roll and eat for lunch, but any extra can be wrapped in parchment paper, then foil, and frozen. Remove foil before thawing and re-heating in the microwave. Pork is a great source of vitamin B1 (vital for muscles) and B12 (for energy)—all good for rolling more burritos!

MAKES 6 BURRITOS

6 Mango or BBQ Gem Wraps

3 cups/630 g Easy and Perfect Sushi Rice (page 128)

½ cup/120 ml Green Slime (page 158)

1 large avocado, pitted, flesh scooped out and thinly sliced

1 cup/225 g shredded, cooked pork (or chicken)

♥ For each wrap, peel plastic backing off Gem Wrap and place, shiny side down, on work surface. Press about ½ cup/105 g of warm rice on lower third of the Gem Wrap. Spoon a generous tablespoon/20 ml of Green Slime across the middle of the rice. Lay a line of avocado slices over Green Slime. Top avocado slices with about 2½ tablespoons/38 g of shredded pork.

♥ Dip a brush into a bowl of cool water, then dab brush onto a towel. Swipe the top border of the Gem Wrap, making sure you get it evenly moistened. Then fold bottom edge of wrap up and around ingredients and roll tightly forward. Let rest on the seam for a minute or two before cutting on the diagonal. Repeat with remaining ingredients.

♥ Serve with Sweeties (page 139) or Bunny Nibbles (page 149) and a side of your favorite green or red salsa.

. . . .

Make sure your rice is warm for this recipe—microwave with a damp paper towel over rice or put in your rice cooker and click the "warm" setting.

CONFETTI BURRITO
VEGGIE FRIED RICE BURRITO WITH CUCUMBERS

This burrito combines the dream team of leftover veggies with last night's sushi rice. Don't worry about the high heat—it's good to get a little caramelization on your veggies and rice, which delivers a rich, nutty flavor. Also, you can freeze leftovers—just take them out of the freezer and move to the fridge the night before.

MAKES 6 BURRITOS

5 cloves garlic, smashed, then peeled

1 onion, roughly chopped

2 carrots, trimmed and peeled, roughly chopped

½ red bell pepper, seeded and roughly chopped

½ yellow or orange bell pepper, seeded and roughly chopped

2 stalks celery, roughly chopped

4 stalks asparagus or green beans, trimmed, roughly chopped

5 scallions, trimmed, roughly chopped

1 tablespoon/15 ml sesame oil

1 tablespoon/15 ml olive oil

4 cups/840 g leftover Easy and Perfect Sushi Rice (page 128)

1 tablespoon/15 ml soy sauce

2 eggs, beaten

6 Gem Wraps, any flavor

¾ cup/180 ml Red Spread (optional; page 156)

½ English cucumber, seeded and cut into ¼" x 4"/0.6 x 10 cm strips (optional)

♥ Put the first 8 ingredients (listed through scallions) in a large food processor and pulse to a finer chop. Remove to a bowl. Feel free to add bits of any other leftover cooked veggies you have on hand (zucchini, mushrooms, corn, spinach, etc.) cut to a similar size. Other yummy "confetti" can be diced pineapple, cashews or tofu.

♥ Heat a large skillet (or wok, if you have one) with sesame and olive oils on high heat. When very hot, add all the veggies and stir-fry for about 4 to 5 minutes, until veggies are seared. Add the soy sauce to the pan, then stir in the rice, and mix together with the vegetables. Let the rice sit still occasionally to get some crispy brown bits on the bottom. Take pan off heat and immediately add the eggs to the rice mixture and stir until egg is cooked, about another minute.

♥ For each burrito, lay Gem Wrap (or tortilla) on work surface and, with a rubber spatula, swipe the lower part of it with 2 tablespoons/30 ml of Red Spread, leaving edges bare. Spoon about ⅔ cup/140 g of rice onto lower third of Red Spread. Lay a few sticks of cucumbers (if using) in the middle of the rice. Roll bottom edge of wrap or tortilla up and around ingredients, grasp tightly and then roll up into a snug roll. Repeat with remaining ingredients. Cut on the diagonal.

♥ Serve with Orange Tamari Sauce (page 166) and lime wedges.

CHICKEN DAWGS
CHICKEN HOT DOGS

Use uncured chicken or turkey dogs for this revamped roll to ensure there are no nitrites, which can be converted into harmful chemicals in the body. The nutritious Gem Wrap can hold a lot more veggies than the average usual mutt, which is usually full of sodium and fat, making this the healthiest hot dog around.

MAKES 4 DOGS

4 uncured chicken or turkey dogs

2 sheets Mango, Tomato, BBQ or Carrot Gem Wrap, each cut in half and then cut to fit length of hot dogs

1 cup/90 g shredded cheddar cheese

2 cups/110 g finely shredded green lettuce or baby spinach

½ cup/75 g thinly sliced red bell peppers

¼ cup/40 g thinly sliced sweet onion (optional)

½ cup/75 g whole kosher dill pickles, thinly sliced into discs

½ cup/120 ml Vampire Sauce (page 165)

Mustard or mayonnaise for dipping

♥ Boil or fry hot dogs until cooked through.

♥ For each wrap, lay Gem Wrap on work surface and sprinkle 1 tablespoon/ 11 g cheese across lower third of wrap. Then scatter ½ cup/27 g lettuce, a few slices of pepper, onion slices (if using) and pickle discs. Cover all with another 1 tablespoon/11 g sprinkle of cheese and top with a hot dog.

♥ Swipe the bare, top border of each Gem Wrap with a wet, but not dripping, brush, making sure you get the wrap border evenly moistened. Roll up tightly and cut each roll into 8 even pieces.

♥ Serve with Vampire Sauce, mustard or mayonnaise, along with Bunny Nibbles (page 149), Sweeties (page 139) and/or Crunchy Pebbles (page 150).

. . . .

Use a mandolin to slice the vegetables quickly and into uniform pieces.

CHAPTER FIVE

RICE WRAPPERS AND BUNS

These beautiful wrappers show off your rolls' feelings—er, fillings—with a translucent glow. Soft and easy to wrap, these are good for rolling any favorite sandwich combo. They're naturally gluten-free and additive-free, making them much healthier than white bread.

Also in this chapter, you'll learn to mold rice into fun shapes like hearts and circles. In Japan, these are called *onigiris*, and they are the favorite snack of children and adults there. They are usually stuffed with a surprise of minced meat, cheese or vegetables and handily wrapped with a sheaf of nori—or here, Gem Wraps! We'll also reconfigure juice boxes into rectangular molds for making rice "buns" to sandwich delicious lunch-box staples.

For some of the recipes in this chapter, you'll need to buy specialty wraps at newgemwraps.com.

TURKEY PEE-WEES
TURKEY REUBEN IN RICE BUN

These are turkey Reubens, but small and funny like PeeWee Herman/Paul Rueben—see? Okay, the kids will LOVE making these with their rice molds or the handy, cut-out juice box (see "How to Make Onigiris," page 169). These rice "sandwiches" are full of calming tryptophan from the turkey and calcium from the Swiss cheese. Your kids will feel double happiness from making their crazy-fun onigiris and eating the nutritious cheering squad they deliver.

MAKES 4-6 REUBENS

Equipment: 2 or 3 snack-size juice boxes with one large side of box cut out. Reserve cut-out for pressing mold.

Plastic wrap for lining box

⅓ cup/80 g mayonnaise

1 tablespoon/30 g sweet pickle relish, finely chopped

Salt and pepper, to taste

2 cups/420 g Easy and Perfect Sushi Rice (page 128)

6 ounces/170 g Swiss cheese, thinly sliced

6 ounces/170 g cooked turkey, thinly sliced

Gem Wraps (your choice of BBQ, Tomato, Mango or Carrot), cut to fit the juice-box mold (use the cut-out box top as a pattern)

♥ Whisk together mayonnaise and relish with salt and pepper to taste and set aside.

♥ Tuck a 12-inch/30-cm piece of plastic wrap into the juice box with sides overhanging. Place one cut piece of Gem Wrap into bottom of box. Fill juice box ⅓ of the way up with rice. Spread 1 tablespoon/15 ml of relish mixture over rice. Follow with a thin slice of cheese and a turkey slice. Then fill in mold with rice to the top. Cover with second cut piece of Gem Wrap. Lay cut-out top of box over Gem Wrap and squeeze the box on all sides to get a tightly pressed sandwich. Turn box upside down and pull on the plastic wrap to unmold the Pee-Wee.

♥ The Pee-Wees can be made the night before and wrapped in parchment or waxed paper. Serve at room temperature or (even better) after a brief flash in the microwave to warm the rice (10 to 15 seconds).

♥ Serve with Crunchy Pebbles (page 150), Bunny Nibbles (page 149) or Alligator Scales (page 143).

RED ROVER

TOMATO AND SALAMI RICE SANDWICH IN TOMATO GEM WRAP

Whip out the trusty juice box and let's make a Red Rover! This sandwich is fun to make and a good-to-eat spin on the ol' bologna and cheese.

MAKES 4 ROVERS

Equipment: 2 snack-size juice boxes with one large side cut out. Reserve the cut-out piece for pressing mold later.

Plastic wrap for lining box

2 Tomato Gem Wraps, cut to fit the juice box mold (use the cut-out box top as a pattern)

2 cups/420 g Easy and Perfect Sushi Rice (page 128)

4 teaspoons/20 ml Red Spread (page 156)

4 thin slices medium tomato, cut in half

8 thin slices salami

♥ Tuck a 12-inch/30-cm piece of plastic wrap into the juice box with sides overhanging. For each sandwich, tuck one cut Gem Wrap piece in the bottom of box. Pack your mold ⅓ of the way up with rice. Spread 1 teaspoon/5 ml of Red Spread evenly on rice. Top with 2 tomato halves end-to-end, then top with salami slices, cut to fit. Top with rice to fill the mold and finish with your Gem Wrap top. Turn box upside down and pull on the plastic wrap to unmold the Rover and serve with Crunchy Pebbles (page 150) or Zucchini Chips (page 146) and pickles.

♥ Also, you can wrap and freeze these Rovers right after you release them from the mold. It's important to freeze them right away, using fresh, warm rice. To defrost, don't let them thaw in the fridge because the rice will lose its texture and become dry. Unwrap the frozen onigiri and put them in a bowl with a damp paper towel on top; then defrost according to your microwave.

PEANUT BUTTER NOODLES
SESAME NOODLE CHICKEN WRAPS

Noodles AND peanut butter? What kid wouldn't mind eating their veggies rolled up in these delicious and fun-to-dip wraps? Rice wrappers and rice noodles guarantee a gluten-free treat that is flavorful and different. And you can roll these in a snap the night before and store on trays under damp paper towels covered with plastic wrap. I double-layer my rice paper wrappers so they don't break when rolling or dipping.

MAKES 4 RICE WRAPS

1 teaspoon/5 ml sesame oil

1 teaspoon/5 ml canola oil

1 clove garlic, minced

2 medium carrots, peeled and finely grated

6 scallions, trimmed and thinly sliced on a diagonal

1 cup/150 g bean sprouts

⅓ cup/42 g cooked chicken, shredded

8 ounces/230 g rice noodles, cooked and rinsed in cold water

1 cup/240 ml Sesame Sauce (page 164)

½ English cucumber, seeded and cut into 4" X ⅛"/10 x 0.3 cm strips

8 8"/20 cm rice paper wrappers

sweet Thai chili sauce for dipping

fresh mango or strawberries for garnish

♥ In a sauté pan, heat both oils over medium heat. Add garlic, carrot, scallions and bean sprouts and cook for about 2 minutes until garlic is fragrant and vegetables are softened. Add chicken and vegetables to cooked rice noodles and toss gently to mix in. Now toss about half of the Sesame Sauce with the noodles and set aside while getting the wrappers ready. Put the other half of the Sesame Sauce in a dipping bowl for later.

♥ In a medium skillet, heat water to hot, but not too hot to dip fingers in. Holding two rice wrappers stacked together, slide them into the hot water to soften, about 1 minute. Keep hold of them at all times, turning them slightly to allow water to penetrate the parts under your fingers.

♥ The wrapper will turn milky and translucent. Remove the wrappers to a damp cutting board, making sure they are still stacked together. Add one-quarter of the sesame noodles in a line across lower third of wrapper. Add cucumber sticks alongside noodles. Wrap lower edge of wrapper up and around ingredients and roll tightly forward. Cut in half on the diagonal. Make remaining rolls with same process. Serve with bottled sweet Thai chili sauce and extra Sesame Sauce for dipping.

♥ Serve with mango and strawberries, Sharky Chips (page 145), Sweeties (page 139) or Origami Crisps (page 140).

DRAGON ROLLS
TEMPURA PORK AND VEGGIE ROLL-UPS

Made with real dragons! Just kidding. A lighter and tastier version of the traditional gluten-heavy egg roll, this Dragon rolls with magic veggie powers.

MAKES 8 RICE WRAPPER ROLLS

1 tablespoon/15 ml tamari

⅛ teaspoon fresh black pepper

½ clove garlic, pressed

1 pound/450 g lean ground pork

5 teaspoons/25 ml sesame oil, divided

6 scallions, trimmed and chopped

2 carrots, finely grated

2 cups/300 g finely shredded cabbage

4 teaspoons/10.7 g grated, fresh ginger

1 clove garlic, pressed

16 small rice paper wrappers

¾ cup/120 g rice flour seasoned with 1 teaspoon/6 g salt and ½ teaspoon ground pepper

2 eggs, beaten

♥ In a bowl, combine tamari, pepper, garlic and pork, and let marinate for 5 to 10 minutes.

♥ In a frying pan or wok, heat 1 tablespoon/15 ml of sesame oil and sauté pork until it's no longer pink, about 1 to 2 minutes. Add scallions, carrots, cabbage, ginger and garlic. Cook 3 minutes until vegetables are just tender. Set aside to cool while preparing rice wrappers.

♥ In a medium skillet, heat water to hot, but not too hot to dip fingers in. Holding two rice wrappers stacked together, slide them into the hot water to soften, about 1 minute. Keep hold of them at all times, turning them slightly to allow water to penetrate the parts under your fingers. The wrapper will turn milky and translucent. Remove the wrappers to a damp cutting board, making sure they are still stacked together.

♥ Spread 2 to 3 tablespoons of the shredded pork mixture in a line across lower third of wrapper. Wrap lower edge of wrapper up and around ingredients and roll tightly forward. Make remaining rolls with same process.

♥ Put seasoned rice flour and beaten egg into separate shallow dishes. Dredge the rolls in the seasoned flour, then the egg, and then the flour again.

♥ Heat the remaining 2 teaspoons/10 ml sesame oil in a large skillet over medium-high heat (350°F/177°C). Fry the Dragon Rolls for 2 minutes, turning a couple of times, until crispy and browned.

♥ Serve with an array of dipping sauces: Vampire Sauce (page 165), bottled sweet Thai chili sauce, Orange Zinger (page 157), and Orange Tamari Sauce (page 166). The colors are fun to look at and add a different dimension to every bite.

♥ Dragon Rolls are featured along with Pichachu Rolls on the photo on page 121.

PICHACHU ROLLS
TEMPURA BEEF AND MUSHROOM ROLL-UPS

Yes, it's a long list of ingredients and steps, but they are all super-easy and fast. Just set it up, watch your little chefs roll, and then fry them. Fry up a whole bunch and freeze them when they cool down.

MAKES 8 RICE WRAPPER ROLLS

1½ cups/225 g thinly sliced, mixed mushrooms (shiitake, brown, white)

1 teaspoon/6.7 g salt and 2 pinches of freshly ground pepper

1 cup/55 g roughly chopped spinach

1 tablespoon/15 ml tamari

1 tablespoon/15 ml black bean sauce

1 pound/450 g flank steak, very thinly sliced

2 teaspoons/10 ml olive oil, divided

1 teaspoon/5 ml toasted sesame oil

16 small, rice paper wrappers

2 eggs, beaten

1 cup/120 g any gluten-free flour, seasoned with salt and pepper

2 cups/475 ml canola oil, for frying

♥ Put sliced mushrooms in a bowl. Sprinkle with salt and pepper, then rub into mushrooms lightly. Let sit for about 2 minutes to release the liquid. Place mushrooms on a double layer of paper towels, twist up into a ball and gently squeeze out water. The mushrooms will be considerably smaller—that's good! Set aside in a bowl. Add spinach and toss.

♥ Mix tamari and black bean sauce in a bowl. Add flank steak and let marinate for 10 minutes.

♥ In a sauté pan, heat the olive oil and sesame oil together until hot. Shake marinade off beef and sauté in oils quickly, about 2 minutes. Remove cooked beef to a bowl next to the mushroom/spinach bowl.

♥ In a medium skillet, heat water to hot, but not too hot to dip fingers in. Holding two rice wrappers together, slide them into the hot water to soften, about 1 minute. Keep hold of them at all times, turning them slightly to allow water to penetrate the parts under your fingers, until they turn milky and translucent. Remove the stacked wrappers to a damp cutting board.

♥ Scatter 1 tablespoon/10 g of mushroom/spinach mixture on lower third of wrapper, leaving a ½-inch/1.3-cm, bare border on all sides. Place one layer of beef slices over the mushroom/spinach. Fold wrapper edge up and over fillings into a tight cylinder. Roll forward halfway to middle of roll. Fold sides in and roll completely forward to seal. Make remaining rolls.

♥ Put flour and beaten egg each into separate shallow dishes. Dredge the Pichachu Rolls in the seasoned flour, then the egg, then the flour again.

♥ Heat the canola oil in a large skillet on medium-high heat. Fry the Pichachu Rolls for 2 minutes, turning, until crispy and browned.

♥ Serve with an array of dipping sauces: Vampire Sauce (page 165), bottled sweet Thai chili sauce, Orange Zinger (page 157) and Orange Tamari Sauce (page 166).

PANDA ROLLS
VEGGIE SPRING ROLLS

Fresh, raw vegetables for lunch? No problem when you dip them in the magic Sesame Sauce. Also, your kids will have fun rolling and creating their own versions of this favorite of pandas everywhere.

MAKES 4 ROLLS

½ pound/230 g thin rice vermicelli

8 8"/20 cm rice paper wrappers

2 cups/110 g finely shredded, green leaf lettuce

1 cup/150 g finely shredded carrot

½ red bell pepper, sliced into matchsticks

1 English cucumber, seeded and cut into ¼" x 4"/0.6 x 10 cm sticks

½ cup/75 g finely chopped, roasted, salted peanuts (optional)

½ cup/120 ml Sesame Sauce (page 164) or bottled sweet Thai chili sauce, for dipping

♥ Bring a large pot of water to boil over high heat. Prepare an ice-water bowl; set aside. Add vermicelli to boiling water and cook just until soft. Drain and immediately dump into the ice-water bowl to cool and stop cooking.

♥ In a medium skillet, heat water to hot, but not too hot to dip fingers in. Holding two rice wrappers together, slide them into hot water to soften, about 1 minute. Keep hold of them at all times, turning them slightly to allow water to penetrate the parts under your fingers. The wrapper will turn milky and translucent. Remove the wrappers to a damp cutting board, making sure they are still stacked together.

♥ Scatter one quarter of the lettuce on lower third of wrapper. Follow with a scatter of carrot, a few matchsticks of red bell pepper and double sticks of cucumber. Sprinkle with a dusting of peanuts (if using).

♥ Wrap lower edge of wrapper up and around ingredients and roll tightly forward. Cut in half on the diagonal. Make remaining rolls with same process.

♥ Serve with Sesame Sauce or sweet Thai chili sauce for dipping and Origami Crisps (page 140), Alligator Scales (page 143) or Bunny Nibbles (page 149) for sidekicks.

ONIGIRIS
RICE MOLDS WITH SHREDDED VEGGIES AND CHEESE

In Japan, rice molds, or *onigiris*, are pressed into plastic molds (see Resources, page 184) and lightly stuffed with tasty surprise, usually salmon or pickled plum, with a strip of nori for a wrapper. My versions feature fun shapes stuffed with hidden wholesomeness. For more help, check out How to Make Onigiris (page 169).

MAKES 4 ONIGIRIS

½ cup/120 ml Golden Spread (page 162)

2 tablespoons/11 g finely shredded Monterey Jack and/or cheddar cheese

2 tablespoons/30 ml sesame oil

½ cup/75 g finely diced broccoli

½ cup/75 g finely diced carrot

2 cups/420 g Easy and Perfect Sushi Rice (page 128)

Salt

4 2" x 4"/5 x 10 cm strips of assorted Gem Wraps flavors (Tomato, Carrot, BBQ) or nori

Green Dream (page 159), Green Slime (page 158) and/or Golden Spread (page 162) for dipping

♥ In a small bowl, mix Golden Spread and cheeses together. Set aside.

♥ Heat sesame oil in a medium sauté pan over medium-high heat. Add broccoli and carrot and sauté until vegetables are just soft, about 5 minutes. Remove from heat and set aside.

♥ Place onigiri mold on work surface. Pack gently with ½ cup/106 g rice. With your little chef's finger, poke a hole into the middle of the mold ¾ of the way down. With a small spoon, pat in some of the cheese mixture and sautéed veggies and cover hole with a little bit of rice. Place onigiri cap on top of the rice and press down. Turn over and, using the thumb slot, push the onigiri out of the mold. Wrap with a strip of Gem Wrap.

OTHER GREAT FILLINGS FOR ONIGIRI INCLUDE:

♥ Chicken salad
♥ Tuna salad
♥ Egg salad
♥ Ham and cheese, minced
♥ Cheddar cheese and minced sweet pickles
♥ Any finely chopped veggies mixed with Schmoo (page 161)
♥ Any minced meat, shrimp or salmon

. . . .

Onigiris freeze very well, if you mold them using fresh, warm rice, then wrap them in plastic wrap right away. This retains moisture to keep the rice texture nice. Let them cool off before placing them in a zipper-lock bag to freeze. To defrost, unwrap the frozen onigiri, put in a bowl with a damp paper towel over it; then defrost according to your microwave instructions. Don't let the rice thaw out before microwaving because the texture will not survive.

CHAPTER SIX

SIDEKICKS AND NIBBLES

What are heroes without their trusty sidekicks who add pop and go the extra mile? Here are some important "Robins", especially the Easy and Perfect Sushi Rice that is featured in many of my rolls. The crispy, salty snap of Crunchy Pebbles and Zucchini Chips gives any wrap or roll extra taste bud-boosting powers. Also, sidekicks can always double as healthy snacks on their own nutritious merit.

EASY AND PERFECT SUSHI RICE
SHORT-GRAINED RICE WITH SUSHI DRESSING

I recommend sushi rice for every white-rice need—not just because I love it the most, but because its pearly grains are easy for Mom to make and perfect for little mouths to eat! It has a different texture from common medium-grain white rice. It has a better "chew" and a smaller grain that makes for better sticking power. Less starchy, it also offers a cleaner taste. It's all-around more delightful than the usual white rice. It holds all of Mom's covert health agents, too, like veggies, spreads and delicious sauces, for extra yum power. A rice cooker is a sure-fire way to cook rice perfectly every time and is a worthy addition to your kitchen gear. Note: Sushi rice requires less water than other white rice, about a 1:1.25 ratio.

MAKES ABOUT 3 CUPS

EQUIPMENT:

1 large, flat-bottomed sieve

1 6–8 cup/1.4–1.9 L rice cooker and rice paddle (comes with rice cooker)

2 cups/400 g premium, short-grain, sushi rice

2¼ cups/535 ml water

Pinch of salt

♥ Pour rice into sieve. Under cold tap water, swish rice around with your fingers until water runs almost clear, about 2 minutes. Place rice and water in the rice cooker and click to the "cook" setting.

♥ In about 20 minutes (or longer, depending on your cooker), the rice cooker will click off. Do not open the lid; let rice rest untouched for about 15 minutes. This is the steaming time and is essential to the rice's perfection.

SCOOBY DOOS
CHICKEN TERIYAKI BITES

These little treats are sweet-tart bites soaked in garlic (a super antibacterial agent) and mineral-rich maple syrup. A delicious lunch treat when rounded out with a few other sidekicks. Make these the night before and freeze a bunch for later, too.

MAKES 10-12 BITES

2 pounds/900 g boneless, skinless chicken thighs

1¾ cups plus 2 tablespoons/475 ml teriyaki sauce

6 tablespoons/90 ml sesame oil

¼ teaspoon minced garlic

Juice of one lemon

2 tablespoons/30 ml maple syrup

2 tablespoons/30 ml canola oil

1 tablespoon/8 g sesame seeds, toasted (optional)

♥ Cut chicken into 2-inch/5-cm pieces. Mix teriyaki sauce and next 4 ingredients (listed through syrup) together in a large zipper-lock bag. Add chicken to bag and marinate for at least 30 minutes or up to overnight.

♥ When ready to cook, take chicken out of marinade (reserve marinade) and let drain in sieve.

♥ In a small saucepan, bring reserved marinade to a boil. Reduce to a simmer for about 15 minutes, or until it thickens. Set aside.

♥ Heat canola oil in a large grill pan over medium-high heat. Grill chicken pieces (in batches if needed to avoid crowding) for about 4 to 5 minutes per side. Brush with the thickened marinade before and after you turn the pieces.

♥ Place cooked chicken in a bowl and pour a little more marinade over chicken to coat, if desired. Toss with sesame seeds, if using. Serve with extra marinade as a dipping sauce. Store in an airtight container in the refrigerator for up to 3 days.

♥ Scooby Doos are great in a lunchbox with Broccoli Trees in Quicksand (page 155) or Felix the Cata-Dillas (page 59). For dinner or lunch at home, serve on skewers for easy dipping.

CUCUMBER BOATS
CUCUMBERS FILLED WITH RICE AND SESAME SAUCE

On a visit with my six-year-old nephew, Stone, we made up this recipe, which is really easy to prepare. Plus, it's fun to tell stories about the boats' many travels as you assemble them. Mine came along the Spice Route; Stone's carried Iron Man on his river-boat vacation. Cucumber boats get around, probably because they transport the energy-giving vitamin B in their hydrating holds. Above decks, they carry pearly sushi rice topped with a bit of Sesame Sauce. Ahoy, tasties!

MAKES 6-8 BOATS

2 English cucumbers, halved and seeds scooped out with a teaspoon

1 cup/210 g Easy and Perfect Sushi Rice (page 128)

¼ cup/60 ml Sesame Sauce (page 164)

Sesame seeds for garnish (optional)

♥ Cut cucumber halves into 3-inch/7.5-cm pieces. On skin sides of the cucumber, slice a thin strip of skin off to make a flat bottom for each "boat" to hold it steady.

♥ Pat in enough rice to just fill the cucumber halves. Drizzle a few drops of Sesame Sauce over the rice and sprinkle lightly with sesame seeds, if using.

HEARTS AND STARS
CUCUMBER AND APPLE SALAD

Here is a sweet and crunchy salad kids will love that delivers a covert, double dose of dietary fiber. This is a perfect side-pairing with almost any Stealth Health wrap, roll or sandwich. In the tasting sessions, we found that cutting the apples and cucumbers into fun shapes like hearts and stars scored high with picky eaters.

MAKES ABOUT 3 CUPS

2 English cucumbers, seeded and sliced into ¼"/0.6 cm thick slices, then cut into shapes with cookie cutters

1 medium green or red apple, seeded and chopped like dice (or sliced into ¼"/0.6 cm-thick slices, then cut into shapes with cookie cutters)

1 teaspoon/6.7 g sea salt, divided

2 teaspoons/10 ml soy sauce or tamari sauce

1 teaspoon/10 ml rice or apple cider vinegar

1 teaspoon/5 ml lemon juice

1 tablespoon/15 ml agave

Sesame seeds or pepitas (optional)

♥ Combine the cucumber and apple in a colander set over the sink and sprinkle with salt. Let sit for about 10 minutes to release some moisture.

♥ In a small bowl, combine the soy sauce, vinegar, lemon juice and agave.

♥ Gently toss drained cucumber and apples with dressing. Add sesame seeds or pepitas (if using), to pack an extra nutritional crunch. Serve as a sidekick in small plastic containers for school lunches.

. . . .

The cucumber and apple cut-outs can be made the day before and stored in separate containers. Just cover the apples with water and 1 teaspoon/5 ml of lemon juice to keep them fresh.

"TASTY AND FRESH! THE DRESSING AND TEXTURE ARE GREAT." —SYLVIE, AGE 12

CRISPY RICE NOODLES

Not stir-fried but crisp-fried, these gluten-free crunchies are super-fast and easy to make. They absorb little oil as they fry, and you can make a bunch and keep them crisp and handy for at least a week in a zipper-lock bag. They're great as a fun snack seasoned with salt.

MAKES ABOUT 5 CUPS OF NOODLES

1 8.8-ounce/250 g package skinny, dried, rice noodles

1 cup/240 ml oil for frying, such as canola, peanut or safflower

Salt, to taste (optional)

♥ Pull apart the sections of the noodles, then thin out the sections. Using scissors, cut the noodles into 4 to 5-inch/10 to 13-cm lengths.

♥ Heat oil in a tall stockpot over medium-high heat for at least 1 minute. (You want the sides of the pan to be high enough to protect from spattering oil.) The key to getting noodles crispy is having the oil hot enough. Test the oil heat by dunking the ends of a few noodles into it. If the oil is hot enough, the submerged parts will "bloom" within seconds into puffy, crispy noodles. If this doesn't happen, wait a few seconds longer, then try again.

♥ Now gently drop handfuls of noodles into the hot oil. Have long tongs at the ready to quickly flip them once and then remove. Cooking time is only a few seconds—they should instantly puff and curl. Set puffed noodles to drain on paper towels and sprinkle with a little salt, if desired. Continue frying the remainder of the noodles.

BARK BITES
CACAO BARS WITH RAW NUTS

Confused about the difference between cacao and chocolate? Cacao is raw chocolate. Out of all the whole foods that contain antioxidants, cacao offers the most. Chocolate bars as we know them are a blend of cacao and varying amounts of sugar and lecithin or butter. Those additives are necessary to temper the cacao—it's quite bitter on its own. But the higher the percentage of cacao (that's what the 70%, 61%, 99%, etc. on the label means), the higher the antioxidant punch. Your kids will love this concoction as much as a commercial chocolate bar, but you, Agent Mom, know the nutrition they're getting when they say "More Bark Bites, please." Wink, wink, nod, nod!

MAKES ABOUT A 12" X 6"/30 X 15-CM RECTANGLE

¼ cup/40 g roughly chopped, raw almonds

¼ cup/40 g sunflower seeds

¼ teaspoon flaky sea salt or pink salt

8 ounces/225 g chopped bittersweet chocolate (with the highest cacao content you can find)

♥ Preheat oven to 250°F/121°C.

♥ Pour almonds and sunflower seeds into a dry skillet and heat over medium-high heat. Toast, stirring for about 1 minute, or until you can smell a toasty nut fragrance. Remove to a bowl, immediately add salt, and stir. Set aside.

♥ Place chocolate in a heat-proof glass bowl and set in oven. Let chocolate melt, stirring occasionally until completely smooth. (I don't like microwaves, but you can also melt the chocolate by heating on high for 30-second intervals, stirring well after each interval.) Pour melted chocolate onto a 2-foot/60-cm piece of parchment paper and smooth out to desired thickness, about ⅛"/0.3 cm.

♥ Sprinkle nut mixture over chocolate. Let stand at room temperature until set (in a safe, secret place) for about an hour. Break off pieces as needed. Store in the refrigerator in a zipper-lock bag, but keep in mind that the bark tastes better at room temperature.

SWEETIES
SWEET POTATO CRISPS

Sweeties are high in vitamins B6, C, and D, iron, potassium and magnesium. And they're super sweet but won't spike insulin like their more common, white-potato cousins do. They are the perfect sidekick to most rolls, AND they're really good dipped in Green Goddess Dressing, Schmoo, Green Slime, Green Dream, Orange Zinger, Grecian Dip, and, and, and....

MAKES ABOUT 3 CUPS OF CHIPS

2 medium, organic, sweet potatoes, peeled

2 tablespoons/30 ml olive oil

1 tablespoon/15 ml soy sauce

1 teaspoon/5 ml lime juice

Salt, to taste

♥ Preheat oven to 300°F/150°C.

♥ With a Y-shaped peeler (see Equipment, page 183) peel sweet potato flesh lengthwise into long strips. Mix olive oil, soy sauce and lime juice, and toss potato slices to coat.

♥ Lay out slices in a single layer on parchment-lined baking sheets and bake for about 1½ hours. Rotate your baking sheets as needed, depending on your oven. When the potatoes start turning golden brown they're almost done—be careful not to over-brown. Sprinkle with a bit of salt immediately after removing from oven. Sweeties will keep for 2 to 3 days in a zipper-lock bag.

ORIGAMI CRISPS

These all-natural, crispy wisps of vegetable squares are made of 100% vegetable purées. They are shiny, colorful and fun to eat. They are tasty alone, or serve them with lots of delicious dips and stealthily healthy spreads. They are a fun and nutritious change from name-brand crackers shaped like orange fish.

MAKES ABOUT 8 CHIPS PER ORIGAMI WRAP

Origami Wraps (Red Bell Pepper, Corn, Carrot and Tomato)

♥ Preheat oven to 190°F/88°C.

♥ With scissors, cut Origami Wraps into 3 x 2-inch/7.6 x 5-cm rectangles or triangles.

♥ Bake the wrap pieces for 25 to 30 minutes, or until crisp. Be careful not to brown, or the chips will taste bitter.

♥ Serve with a couple of (or many!) dipping sauces, or dollop a little spread on crisps and serve like crackers.

TRY THESE FOR DIPPING:

♥ Schmoo (page 161)
♥ Green Slime (page 158)
♥ Orange Zinger (page 157)
♥ Quicksand (page 155)
♥ Golden Spread (page 162)
♥ Green Goddess Dressing (page 163)
♥ Grecian Dip (page 160)

ALLIGATOR SCALES
MISO-HONEY KALE CHIPS

Kale is a genuine, stealthy health food, and it beats the curls out of cheese puffs for a crunchy snack. It offers more iron than beef, more calcium than milk, and your required daily allowance of omega-3s, all in a crispy, green jacket. Kids love the savory chips, and the fact that they can help prepare them makes them even more fun to eat. Make a double batch and keep in airtight containers for up to five or six days. Experiment with other seasonings to discover your family's fave flavors—try lemon-pepper, parmesan cheese or seasoned salt.

MAKES 2 TO 3 CUPS

1 large bunch green kale (curly or Tuscan is fine)

1 heaping tablespoon/15 ml white miso paste

1 tablespoon/15 ml soy sauce

2 teaspoons/10 ml lemon juice

2 tablespoons/30 ml honey

2 tablespoons/30 ml olive oil

♥ Preheat oven to its lowest setting, around 150°F/66°C.

♥ Separate kale bunch and wash leaves thoroughly. Trim all thick veins from the kale and tear leaves into approximately 3 x 3-inch/7.6 x 7.6-cm pieces. Spin in a salad spinner to get leaves very dry. This is important, allowing sauce to cling to leaves, which permits leaves to crisp. If you don't have a salad spinner, then pat leaves dry with a paper towel.

♥ Combine the remaining ingredients in a bowl and mix until blended well. Place dry kale leaves in a large bowl and use your hands to toss the kale with enough miso sauce just to coat evenly (you may have extra sauce left over). It's all fun for little chefs, playing with goo and food.

♥ Spread kale leaves in a single layer on greased baking sheets and bake about 1½ to 2 hours, or until the leaves are crispy. Check occasionally and turn baking sheets around in oven at least once.

RAW ALLIGATOR CHIPS

These chips cook at an even lower temperature than Alligator Scales, and for a long, long time, but this preserves the enzymes and nutrients in the kale that cooking at higher temps knocks out.

♥ Preheat oven to 115°F/46°C (if possible), or use a dehydrator if you have one. Prepare kale as directed for Alligator Scales and season to taste. Bake for about 5 to 6 hours.

. . . .

Dehydrators are cool. You can dehydrate so many things, like fruit slices, veggie slices or meats. Season them as you like and keep them for weeks as über-nutritious snacks. They retain their nutrients because dehydration doesn't destroy their original enzymes and vitamins.

SHARKY CHIPS
TEMPURA SEAWEED CRISPS

Nori is the most nutritious of all the seaweeds, with an amazing 30% to 50% of protein from amino acids and more vitamin C than oranges. Kids will love the crispy umami taste and can help with the dusting and battering duties. Try them dipped in sweet teriyaki or Thai chili sauce for a snack that will beat out corn chips every time.

MAKES ABOUT 16–20 CHIPS

1 egg

1 cup/240 ml ice-cold water

1 cup/120 g rice flour, plus extra for dusting

4 sheets nori, cut into 4" x 2"/10 x 5 cm strips, toasted

3 cups/710 ml canola or safflower oil, for deep frying

♥ To make the batter, whisk the egg with the ice-cold water. Add the flour and stir (batter will be lumpy).

♥ Heat oil in a deep pan to 325°F/163°C.

♥ Dust seaweed strips with a little rice flour and then drag the strips through the batter. Fry immediately for 2 minutes, until golden.

♥ Serve immediately with lemon slices, or cool completely and store in zipper-lock bags to keep for up to 2 weeks.

ZUCCHINI CHIPS

CRISPY ZUCCHINI CHIPS WITH SEA SALT

Rice crumbs and brown rice flour give a nutty crunch to these super-healthy chips. One cup of zucchini has 10% of the Recommended Daily Allowance of fiber and high levels of vitamins A and C. These are an excellent alternative to potato chips or cheese crackers, and they taste great with Grecian Dip (page 160) and/or Golden Spread (page 162) as dippers.

MAKES ABOUT 30–40 CHIPS

2 cups/475 ml canola or safflower oil

1 cup/110 g brown rice flour

1 teaspoon/6.7 g fine sea salt

½ teaspoon black pepper

½ teaspoon garlic powder

1 large egg, beaten

2 teaspoons/10 ml whole milk

1 cup/150 g rice crumbs

2 medium zucchini, thinly sliced on a slight diagonal and patted dry

♥ In a medium skillet, heat the oil to 350°F/177°C.

♥ Meanwhile, in a shallow dish, combine brown rice flour, salt, pepper and garlic powder. Whisk egg with milk and put into a second shallow dish; place rice crumbs in a third shallow dish.

♥ Dip each zucchini slice into the flour mixture, then the egg, and finally the rice crumbs. Set on a rack while you finish dredging the rest of the zucchini slices.

♥ Fry zucchini chips until they are golden brown, about 70 to 90 seconds. Remove the chips with a slotted spoon and drain on paper towels to absorb excess oil.

· ·

Use a mandolin to slice the zucchini quickly into thin, even slices for chips.

BUNNY NIBBLES

CARROT CRISPS WITH GREEN GODDESS DRESSING

Carrots! Everyone knows, especially bunnies, the delights of the crunchy, sweet, juicy blast that carrots kick around in your mouth. They're high in fiber, vitamin A and beta carotene. What's better for dipping than raw carrots? Bunny Nibbles! Paired with Green Goddess Dressing, you have a "garden-variety" hit on your healthy kids' hands.

MAKES ABOUT 30–40 LONG CHIPS

2 large carrots (at least 1"/2.5 cm in diameter), peeled

1½ teaspoons/7.5 ml olive oil

½ teaspoon sea or pink salt

½ cup/120 ml Green Goddess Dressing, for dipping (page 163)

♥ Preheat oven to 200°F/107°C.

♥ With a Y-shaped vegetable peeler (see Equipment, page 183), shave the carrots into thin, even slices. Place the carrot strips in a medium bowl, add the oil and salt to taste, and toss with your hands until thoroughly coated. Place the strips in a single layer on 2 baking sheets lined with parchment paper. Allow the strips to touch but not overlap.

♥ Bake for 45 minutes, and then rotate the pans between the racks. Bake until the edges of the chips are just turning golden brown, about 45 minutes more. Let crisps cool before serving with a dipping bowl of Green Goddess Dressing.

♥ Store in an airtight container for up to 5 days.

CRUNCHY PEBBLES
BAKED CHICKPEAS

These crafty crunchies supply dietary fiber and amino acids. They are the perfect sidekick for most roll-ups and are ideal for your cocktail parties, so make extra! Your little chefs can help you pick off loose skins and toss the chickpeas in olive oil with their little chef hands. Crunchy Pebbles are great for lunch-box snacks and after-school energy boosters. See who eats them faster—you or your kids.

MAKES 1 CUP/165 G

1 16-ounce/450 g can chickpeas (also called garbanzos)

2 teaspoons/10 ml olive oil

Dusting of paprika (optional)

Sea salt or Kosher salt, to taste

♥ Preheat oven to 400°F/204°C.

♥ Drain and wash the chickpeas. Lay out a dry kitchen towel and roll chickpeas around with your hand to dry them. This will free some loose outer skins, but they crisp up nicely. Pat dry, dry, dry. (The drier the chickpea, the crispier the "pebble.")

♥ Put dry chickpeas in a large bowl and drizzle with olive oil. Dust with paprika, if desired. Spread chickpeas over a silicone baking mat or some parchment paper fitted to a rimmed baking sheet.

♥ Cook for 15 to 20 minutes and then turn baking sheet around in the oven, giving the "pebbles" a good rattle on the way. Continue to cook for another 15 minutes, or until chickpeas are firm and crispy. If they aren't crispy, keep them baking. Remove from oven and immediately sprinkle with salt. I find they can take a lot of seasoning.

♥ Let cool and keep in an airtight container for up to 10 days.

CHAPTER SEVEN

DIPS AND SPREADS

As I said before, if you dip it, they will eat it! And these spreads are the powerhouse nutrition-carriers of many—maybe most—of my stealth tricks. They're better than Mary Poppins' "spoonful of sugar to make the medicine go down," but it's the same idea. The Golden and Red Spreads carry a few tablespoons of herbs and vegetables packed into cream cheese goodness in each bite. The dips are rich in fresh vegetables that are concentrated purées hidden behind savory seasonings. So give them a Bunny Nibble or Alligator Scale to scoop with, and watch the nutrients go down with smiles.

BROCCOLI TREES IN QUICKSAND
CAULIFLOWER HUMMUS WITH BROCCOLI DIPPERS

Broccoli is high in vitamin C, and a remarkable 45% of its calories come from protein. But your little guys will just think they are the coolest edible "trees" around. Spread the hummus out on a big platter and, besides your broccoli "trees," have on hand sprout "grass," shredded carrot "bushes" and almond and sunflower seed "stones." Your little landscapers can create their own garden of yummy delights!

MAKES ABOUT 2 CUPS OF HUMMUS

STEAMED BROCCOLI "TREES"

½ **bunch broccoli**

water and ice for an ice bath

QUICKSAND

½ **head cauliflower, stemmed and broken up into large florets**

1 **clove garlic, pressed**

2 **tablespoons/30 ml tahini sauce**

1 **tablespoon/15 ml lemon juice**

¼ **cup/60 ml olive oil**

2 **teaspoons/13 g sea salt, or to taste**

♥ For the broccoli "trees," rinse broccoli and cut off the stem at about 2 inches/5 cm above the base. Cut out bite-sized florets, trimming each floret stem flat across.

♥ Bring ¾ to 1 inch/2 to 2.5 cm of water to a boil in a saucepan with a steamer insert. Add the broccoli to the steamer, or simply put the broccoli directly into the boiling water, and cover. Reduce heat to medium and let cook for 4 to 5 minutes, being careful not to overcook. Make an ice bath with 4 cups/960 ml of water and 1 tray of ice cubes. Plunge cooked broccoli into ice bath. This stops the cooking and makes your "trees" pop with green.

♥ To make quicksand, steam cauliflower like you steamed the trees, but do not use an ice bath. Place cauliflower and remaining ingredients in a blender and purée.

Quicksand is also good with Origami Crisps (page 140), gluten-free pita chips and fresh vegetable and apple sticks.

RED SPREAD
RED BELL PEPPER DIP

This is one of my super stars that will lead your child's taste buds down many clandestine, healthy paths. Packed with almost 2 cups/200 g of red bell pepper-vitamin C pow, Red Spread tastes so good with fresh veggie sticks or on rice crackers and Origami Chips. But the stealth genius comes when you can tuck in other super foods like salmon, chopped spinach and tomatoes. Based on calcium-rich cream cheese and feta, you can't find a tastier undercover agent than Red Spread.

MAKES ABOUT 2 CUPS (480 ML)

2 fresh red bell peppers, lightly roasted, seeded and peeled (or 4–5 ounces/117–145 g of jarred, roasted red bell pepper)

16 ounces/900 g cream cheese

5 ounces/140 g feta cheese, crumbled

1 teaspoon/5 ml water

½ teaspoon fresh lemon juice

Sea salt and pepper, to taste

♥ Place all ingredients in a blender or food processor and blend until smooth. Chill to set before using.

ORANGE ZINGER

CARROT GINGER DIP

Think your kid won't touch raw veggies? Try this sweet-tangy dip with bright sticks of yellow, orange and red bell pepper, cucumber and cauliflower florets, and watch them disappear. Also good with Zucchini Chips, this all-raw vegetable snack is a powerhouse of live enzymes and vitamins, but your kid will just think it's like eating a rainbow.

MAKES 1½ CUPS/360 ML

½ cup/120 g mayonnaise

¼ cup/60 g cream cheese

3 teaspoons/15 ml seasoned rice vinegar

1 teaspoon/5 ml orange juice

1 tablespoon/15 ml soy sauce

¼ teaspoon sesame oil

5 medium carrots, chopped

2 tablespoons/16 g peeled ginger, chopped

2 scallions, tough green ends trimmed, chopped

♥ Place all ingredients in a blender and purée for a couple of minutes. Place in an airtight container and chill. Orange Zinger will stay good for a week of dipping goodness.

"I WANT MORE ORANGE, MOMMY!" —ELLA, AGE 3

GREEN SLIME
AVOCADO BUTTER

Avocados pack more than 25 essential nutrients, and the tiny kick of the jalapeño slyly adds almost 10% of the recommended daily value of vitamin C. Use as a healthier alternative to mayonnaise or as a delicious dip for after-school veggie sticks and whole-grain crackers. Slip the Slime to your kids!

MAKES ABOUT 1½ CUPS/360 ML

2 ripe avocadoes, pitted and skinned

½ cup/56 g sour cream or plain yogurt (for more tang)

3 tablespoons/7.5 g chopped basil (6–7 leaves)

½ cup/15 g roughly chopped spinach

2 teaspoons/10 ml fresh lime juice

½ jalapeño, seeded and minced (optional)

Sea salt and black pepper, to taste

♥ Purée all ingredients in a blender or mini food processor until smooth.

♥ Add water to thin, if needed.

"MELTS IN MY MOUTH!" –SOPHIE, AGE 7

GREEN DREAM
GREEN CASHEW AIOLI

This dip is a double-happiness dream of garlic, which wards off bacterial bugs (as well as vampires), and raw foods that help the body stay full of alkaline electrons, so little batteries stay super-charged. They don't need to know all that (except maybe the vampire part), but you can feel good about delivering a dream as green as this.

MAKES ABOUT 1 CUP/240 ML

½ cup/150 g raw cashews

¼ cup/60 ml water

2 cups/80 g basil leaves

½ cup/15 g roughly chopped spinach leaves

1 cup/40 g fresh cilantro leaves (optional)

¼ cup/10 g fresh mint leaves (optional)

3 tablespoons/45 ml lemon juice

1 tablespoon/17 g white miso paste

1 small clove fresh garlic, pressed

½ teaspoon sea salt, to taste

♥ Purée all ingredients until smooth. Add water to thin, if needed.

♥ Serve with fresh cut veggies like cucumber, carrots and celery. Serve with chips like Origami Crisps (page 140), Sweeties (page 139) and Bunny Nibbles (page 149).

GRECIAN DIP
CUCUMBER YOGURT DIP

Aaaah, the Greeks! They have one of the world's healthiest diets and are among the longest-lived populations. This stealthy dose of bone-building calcium will keep your young ones growing strong and long.

MAKES ABOUT 2 CUPS/480 ML

½ cup/75 g English cucumber, seeded but not peeled

½ cup/45 g feta cheese, finely crumbled

¾ cup/184 g plain, low-fat yogurt

1 tablespoon/15 ml lemon juice

½ small clove garlic, pressed

½ teaspoon salt

Pinch of pepper

♥ Grate cucumber on a box grater into the middle of a double layer of paper towels. Twist up ends of towels and squeeze shredded cucumber into a tight ball to press out excess liquid. Place in a small bowl. Add the remaining ingredients and mix gently. Let chill for 30 minutes before serving. You can keep Grecian Dip in an airtight container in the fridge for up to 4 days.

SCHMOO
PESTO CREAM CHEESE SPREAD

I promise, whatever you put this spread on, in, or around will get eaten! Kids will love the cheesy goodness, but you will love the big green daddies of antioxidants—spinach, basil and parsley—packed into every tablespoon. Make a big batch that will work all week on sandwiches and snacks and for dips. You can also freeze in portions and, after thawing, just re-blend to restore the texture.

MAKES ABOUT 2 CUPS/480 ML

1 cup/55 g roughly chopped, fresh spinach

¾ cup/30 g roughly chopped, fresh basil

½ cup/20 g roughly chopped, fresh parsley, any kind

½ cup/45 g grated Parmesan cheese

2 cups/464 g cream cheese

½ teaspoon salt

1 teaspoon/5 ml lemon juice

½ clove garlic, pressed

♥ Place all ingredients in blender and blend until smooth. Place in an airtight container and keep refrigerated for up to a week.

"I THINK THIS KEEPS AWAY THE BAD GUYS, MOMMY." —VERA, AGE 4

GOLDEN SPREAD
CARROT CREAM CHEESE

Try Golden Spread instead of mayonnaise or processed cheese slices. Spread on everything from Chinese Chicken Rolls (page 44) to Unicorn Rolls (page 55) to add a burst of flavor and carrot-goodness to all your little ones' lunches. Great for a spread on crackers, or use it as a dip for fresh cucumber and bell pepper sticks.

MAKES ABOUT 1½ CUPS/360 ML

2 large carrots, peeled and finely grated

½ small, red, bell pepper, fresh or roasted and chopped

8 ounces/227 g cream cheese, cubed

½ cup/75 g feta cheese, crumbled

½ teaspoon olive oil

Salt, to taste

Warm water to thin, if needed

♥ Place grated carrots in the middle of double-layered paper towels. Twist paper towel corners up to form grated carrots into a ball and squeeze water out.

♥ Add squeezed carrots to blender with the rest of the ingredients and purée until smooth. Add salt, if desired, and thin with warm water, if necessary.

. . . .

One medium carrot provides more than 200% of the recommended daily allowance of vitamin A.

"I LIKE TO DIP IN THE BROCCOLI! YOU SHOULD CALL IT 'GOLDEN DIP.'" —CHARLES, AGE 9

GREEN GODDESS DRESSING
FRESH GREEN HERB, GARLIC AND SOUR CREAM DRESSING

The Green Goddess is a fantastic creamy dip for chips, crisps or nibbles. Adults can always use it as a trusty stand-by salad dressing or dip for cocktail canapés. What if you said to your kid, "Here's a spoonful of concentrated spinach, basil, parsley, avocado, garlic and lemon juice with a touch of anchovy. Want a bite?" Luckily, all you have to say is, "Need a little Green Goddess to dip that in?" and the answer will be, "Yes, please!"

MAKES ABOUT 1 CUP/240 ML

½ cup/20 g parsley leaves

½ cup/15 g baby spinach

¼ cup/10 g basil leaves, roughly chopped

½ small clove garlic, mashed to a paste, with salt

¼ cup/50 g sour cream

½ cup/120 g mayonnaise

½ avocado, peeled and seeded

1 teaspoon/5 ml fresh lemon juice

1 teaspoon/5 ml water

½ teaspoon anchovy paste (optional)

Sea salt and fresh black pepper, to taste

♥ Place all dressing ingredients in a blender and purée until smooth. Dressing will keep for 3 to 4 days in the refrigerator.

SESAME SAUCE
PEANUT BUTTER, SESAME OIL AND GINGER SAUCE

Deep within this yummy peanut butter taste is sly sesame oil (full of healing magnesium), cleansing ginger, and apple cider with sweet ol' honey. This sauce is great tossed with rice noodles, on warm sushi rice, and as a dip for carrots, jicama, celery, bell peppers, spring rolls...; kids big and small will pretty much eat whatever you sauce or dip it with.

MAKES ABOUT 1 CUP/240 ML

½ cup/130 g smooth peanut butter

3 tablespoons/45 ml soy sauce

⅓ cup/80 ml warm water

2 teaspoons/5.3 g fresh ginger, peeled and finely grated

1½ tablespoons/22.5 ml seasoned rice vinegar

1 tablespoon/15 ml toasted sesame oil

1 tablespoon/15 ml apple cider

2 teaspoons/10 ml honey

♥ Place all ingredients in a blender and blend to a smooth paste. Will keep in the refrigerator for up to 2 weeks.

"THIS SAUCE IS YUMMY BECAUSE IT TASTES LIKE PEANUT BUTTER SAUCE!"
—CHARLOTTE, AGE 8

VAMPIRE SAUCE
FRESH TOMATO KETCHUP

Homemade ketchup is so good and so easy to make. Yes, some straining is involved, but you can make a batch that will last a long while. You'll be happy because this recipe avoids all the additives and high-fructose corn syrups of most commercial brands of ketchup (and the cooking process doesn't lessen the super-antioxidant powers of tomatoes' lycopene), but your kids will be grinning and dipping because of the fresh taste.

MAKES ABOUT 1¼ CUPS/300 ML

4 cups/600 g ripe grape or cherry tomatoes

1 cup/240 ml seasoned rice vinegar

⅓ cup/60 g dark brown sugar

3 teaspoons/20 g salt

1 teaspoon/6.7 g black pepper

⅛ teaspoon onion powder

1 teaspoon/5 ml hoisin sauce

♥ In a large food processor, pulse tomatoes briefly, just to break the skins (do not purée).

♥ In a large skillet over medium-low heat, simmer tomatoes, vinegar, sugar, salt, pepper and onion powder until sauce thickens like jam, about 20 minutes. Let sauce cool slightly, then purée in food processor until smooth. Strain through a mesh sieve, then strain again (to get a finer texture). Stir in hoisin sauce and chill.

♥ Will keep refrigerated for up to 3 weeks.

ORANGE TAMARI SAUCE
WHEAT-FREE SOY SAUCE

This sultry tamari sauce includes a spark of fresh orange juice to make a special dipping sauce for all your sushi rolls and Chinese wraps.

MAKES 2 CUPS/480 ML

1 tablespoon/6.5 g raw sugar

½ cup/120 ml water

6 tablespoons/90 ml orange juice

1 cup/240 ml tamari sauce

♥ In a bowl, mix sugar and water until sugar dissolves. Add orange juice and tamari sauce and mix well. Store in refrigerator up to 2 weeks.

QUICK TOMATO SAUCE
FRESH AND FAST TOMATO SAUCE

Why buy expensive store-bought tomato sauce when you can whip up a tastier and healthier homemade version in minutes? Packed with vitamins A, C and K and skin-enriching lycopene, every spoonful of this tomato sauce is like a nourishing vitamin pill of tangy goodness.

MAKES 2 CUPS/480 ML

2 cups/300 g grape tomatoes

1 clove garlic, pressed

2 leaves fresh basil, torn up

2 tablespoons/30 ml olive oil

Salt and pepper, to taste

♥ Place tomatoes, garlic, basil, salt and pepper in a food processor and blend to a purée.

♥ Heat olive oil in a skillet over medium heat. Add tomato purée and cook on a simmer for 15 minutes. Adjust seasoning if needed.

HOW TO COOK PERFECT SUSHI RICE

Pour measured rice into sieve. Under cold tap water, swish rice around with your fingers until water runs almost clear, about 2 minutes.

Place rice in a rice cooker and fill with water until it is 1 inch/2.5 cm above rice. Or measure 1 part rice to 1.25 parts water. Click the "cook" setting (careful—there is sometimes a "warmer" setting too, which you don't want to click at the beginning.)

In about 30 to 40 minutes, depending on your particular cooker, it will click off. Do not open the lid; let rice rest untouched for about 15 minutes. This is the steaming time and is essential to the rice's success.

Then open lid and fluff with rice paddle (included with the rice cooker), releasing steam and loosening rice grains. Pour sushi dressing over paddle to distribute evenly, and then cut dressing into rice to mix.

HOW TO MAKE ONIGIRIS

FOR ONIGIRIS:

Place onigiri mold on work surface. Pack gently with rice. With your finger, poke a hole into the middle of the mold ¾ of the way down. Use a small spoon to pat in some minced ingredients, and cover hole with a little bit of rice. Place onigiri cap on top and press down to mold. Turn over, and using the thumb slot, push the onigiri out of the mold. Wrap with a strip of desired Gem Wrap flavor.

FOR JUICE-BOX MOLDS:

Cut out one long side of a snack-size juice box, reserving the cut-out piece for pressing mold later. Line juice box with plastic wrap, letting sides overhang.

For each rice bun, use the cut-out piece of juice box as a pattern to cut two pieces of Gem wrap. Place one Gem Wrap piece in the bottom of juice box. Pack your mold ⅓ way up the sides with rice.

Dollop 1 teaspoon/5 ml of Red Spread (page 156) on rice and spread evenly. Cover with 2 layers of each of the other ingredients (cut them to fit the box size, if necessary). Top with rice to fill the mold, and press down with the cut-out piece of juice box. Flip over and pull on the plastic wrap to unmold. Top with your Gem Wrap top.

HOW TO ROLL A CATERPILLAR ROLL

Chop the skinny end of the carrot into 10 to 12 small, thin discs. These are the eyes and spots of your pet bug. Now cut carrot in half lengthwise. Lay flat side down and trim off 4 long, slender strips that get thinner at one end. These will be the antennae. Set aside.

Hold half of an avocado in the palm of your hand and, with a tablespoon, scoop out the flesh, keeping it in one whole piece. Set it hole-side down and cut it crosswise into very thin slices. (Avocado can be tricky to work with. It is easiest to slice by putting your knife tip 2"/5 cm above the avocado half and pulling the knife through the flesh.)

Cover your sushi rolling mat with plastic wrap. Place one nori sheet on the rolling mat. Wet hands and spread about ½ cup/105 g of Easy and Perfect Sushi Rice (page 128) evenly over entire nori. Flip the nori sheet over and arrange on mat, allowing a ½"/1.3 cm border between bottom edge of mat and long bottom edge of nori. Place two double sticks of cucumber in a line across the middle of the nori. Roll forward using mat and let roll rest on its seam for at least 1 minute to seal. Repeat to form remaining roll.

Now, slide a long knife under one sliced avocado half and place it on top of the sushi roll, fanning it out (like dominoes) to fit from one end to the other. Take a sheet of plastic wrap and cover the roll. Place the sushi mat over the roll and give it a gentle squeeze to allow the avocado to adhere to the rice.

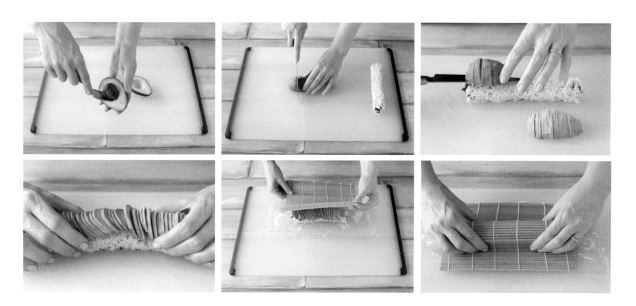

Remove mat and, leaving plastic wrap in place, cut through plastic into 8 even pieces. You need a very sharp knife for this or else it will squash the bug. Gently pull off the plastic wrap. Now the little chefs can come in and decorate.

Place carrot eyes appropriately and then arrange spots in rows down the caterpillar's back. Stick in two carrot antennae near his head. Sprinkle on "freckles" of sesame seeds if desired.

HOW TO ROLL A GEM WRAP

Peel plastic backing off Gem Wrap and place, shiny side down, on work surface.

Wet and dab hands partly dry, then pat sushi rice (if using) over Gem Wrap in an even layer (about 3 to 4 grains thick), leaving a 2-inch/5-cm bare border at the top. Add remaining ingredients in an even line across lower third of rice.

If not using rice, arrange ingredients in required amounts across lower third of Gem Wrap.

Dip a natural-bristled brush into a bowl of cool water (rubber brushes don't spread water evenly), then dab onto a towel to remove dripping water. You want the moisture to be like licking a stamp—not too wet, not too dry.

Swipe the top border of the Gem Wrap, making sure you get it evenly moistened all the way across. Any dry spots will not adhere (again, like a stamp). If you get it too wet, it will pucker and tear, and you'll probably have to re-do it. You'll get a feel for it in no time!

Roll lower edge of Wrap up and around ingredients and roll over tightly. If using a sushi mat (which always gives you a tighter roll, but it's not necessary), roll over until you touch top of the rice, and, holding mat tightly, release leading edge of mat before rolling to close the roll.

Let rest on the seam for a minute or two before cutting on the diagonal.

IF USING RICE:

IF NOT:

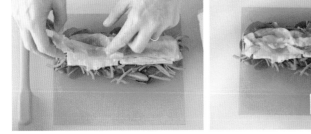
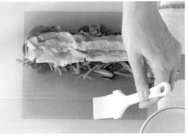

HOW TO ROLL A GEM WRAP PINWHEEL

Peel plastic backing from Gem Wrap.

Arrange ingredients in single layers, leaving a 3-inch/7.5-cm border at the top. Wet brush and dab on towel to get excess water off.

Swipe the border with the damp brush, making sure the border is evenly moistened all the way across.

Crimp leading edge of Gem Wrap and begin to roll forward, pulling ingredients into wrap as you roll forward. Finish rolling Gem Wrap and let rest on the seam for at least 1 minute to hydrate and seal.

Cut Gem Wrap into 8 even pieces, with firm sawing motions, and double wrap "to go" in parchment paper and foil. (Plastic wrap will make the Wrap retain too much moisture and become soggy.)

HOW TO ROLL A SUSHI ROLL

SUSHI WITH NORI:

Some recipes call for a whole sheet of nori and some for half-sheets. For a half-sheet of nori, simply cut a whole nori sheet in half. First, hold up a full sheet of nori and note the pressed lines running across the surface. Then, fold sheet in half, parallel to those lines. Run a knife along the crease to split the nori into a clean half. Stack these half-sheets on a plate. Store unused ones in a zipper-lock bag.

Prepare a finger bowl of cold water (I put ice cubes in mine—the cooler the hands, the less sticky the rice) for wetting your fingers and palms. Next to the water bowl, always have your trusty, folded kitchen towel, on which to tap off excess water and rice from your fingers.

Take your new friend, the rolling mat, and place it green-side up, with the slats running horizontally and the little white string ends at the top. Place the nori half-sheet with the smoother, shinier side down, horizontally on your rolling mat (with the pressed lines in the nori running the same way as the slats in the mat). It is very important to always make sure that the bottom edge of the nori is 3 to 4 slats above the bottom edge of the mat. It sounds ridiculously exact, but trust me—there are sushi angels in the details.

Wet your palms and fingers and tap your fingers on your towel so you're not dripping. Scoop out the required amount of sushi rice. Form it into a very loose ball about the size of a plum. Place the rice ball in the center of the nori. With your fingertips, gently tap down the rice ball and spread the rice over the nori, leaving a bare, 1-inch/2.5-cm border across the top of the nori sheet. Smooth over any lumps and fill any holes in the surface of the rice layer, which should be about 3 grains thick.

The roll is now ready for ingredients. Most ingredients will be cut into 4" x ¼"/10 x 0.6-cm strips or added in quantities of about 2 tablespoons/30 ml.

Place ingredients across the lower third of the rice. Be sure not to overlap the filling ingredients in the middle; otherwise your roll will have an unsightly bulge and be hard to close.

Hook your thumbs under lower edge of the mat and, with your other fingers, hold in ingredients as you roll the edge up and around them. Roll over until the leading edge of the mat closes over the rice edge at the top of nori. You should be able to see your 1-inch/2.5-cm, bare border. Squeeze along the length of the mat to shape and tighten the roll.

Do not loosen your grip—don't squish your roll, either; just apply a firm, constant pressure so the roll won't spring open. Now, lift the edge of the mat slightly, letting it slide forward (so you don't roll the mat into the roll), and continue rolling forward to close the roll. Squeeze the length of the mat again. Remove the roll from the mat and place onto the cutting board.

Dip the point of a very sharp knife into the bowl of water and upend the knife to allow water to run down the blade.

Start with the knife point poised over the middle of roll at a 45-degree angle. Using sure sawing motions, slice the roll in half. Horizontally stack the two half pieces side by side. Holding roll halves together, make two evenly spaced cuts through them, resulting in half being cut into thirds. Wet and wipe knife between cuts. (You'll get into the habit of wetting and wiping, and wetting and wiping your knife. It really makes the cutting clean and easy.)

Serve pieces of sushi roll with small dishes of dipping sauce on the side.

Troubleshooting: If seam won't stay closed, leave roll on mat and gently scrape out some rice from the top edge and discard, or cut ingredients into more slender strips.

SUSHI ROLLS WITH ORIGAMI:

Follow the same directions as above, except swipe the bare border of the Origami Wrap with a wet, but not dripping, brush before you roll it up.

HOW TO ROLL AN INSIDE-OUT ROLL

Some recipes call for a whole sheet of nori and some for half-sheets. For a half-sheet of nori, simply cut a whole nori sheet in half. First, hold up a full sheet of nori and note the pressed lines running across the surface. Then, fold sheet in half, parallel to those lines. Run a knife along the crease to split the nori into a clean half. Stack these half sheets on a plate. Store unused ones in a zipper-lock bag.

Prepare a finger bowl of cold water (I put ice cubes in mine—the cooler the hands, the less sticky the rice) for wetting your fingers and palms. Next to the water bowl, always have your trusty, folded kitchen towel, on which to tap off excess water and rice from your fingers.

Take the rolling mat and cover it with plastic wrap so your inside-out roll won't stick to the mat. Now place it green-side up, with the slats running horizontally and the little white string ends at the top. Place the nori half-sheet horizontally on your mat. It is very important to always make sure that the bottom edge of the nori is 3 to 4 slats above the bottom edge of the mat. It sounds ridiculously exact, but trust me—there are sushi angels in the details.

Wet your palms and fingers and tap your fingers on your towel so you're not dripping. Scoop out the required amount of sushi rice. Form it into a very loose ball about the size of a plum. Place the rice ball in the center of the nori. With your fingertips, gently tap down the rice ball and spread the rice over the entire surface of the nori. Sprinkle with seeds or nuts, if using.

Grasp the top, upper corners of the nori sheet and flip it toward you, arranging the nori so there is ½ inch/1.3 cm between the bottom edge of the nori and the bottom edge of the mat. This is very important to the success of the rolling process.

Now lay your filling ingredients in a line across the bottom third of the nori. Roll the nori up with the mat, curling the bottom edge of the mat up and around the ingredients. Pause here, still firmly holding the mat in place, and slightly lift the leading edge of the mat to let it roll up forward (so the mat won't roll up into the roll). Finish rolling the nori forward again to close the roll. Cut into 8 even pieces and serve with your favorite dipping sauce.

HOW TO ROLL WITH RICE WRAPPERS

In a medium skillet, heat water to hot, but not too hot to dip fingers in. Turn heat off when water gets hot enough. Holding two rice wrappers together, slide them into hot water to soften—this will take about 1 minute. Keep hold of the wrappers at all times, turning wrappers slightly to allow water to penetrate the parts under your fingers.

The wrapper will turn milky and translucent. Remove the two wrappers, making sure they are still stacked together, to a damp cutting board or a damp kitchen towel on a cutting board.

Arrange filling ingredients across lower third of wrap. Roll bottom edge up and over ingredients and roll forward for one turn. Tuck in side edges and then continue to roll up to close.

PANTRY AND EQUIPMENT

PANTRY

Black bean sauce—This sauce, made from salted black beans, can be used to flavor anything from dipping sauces to stir-fries to braised dishes. You can store open jars in the fridge for up to a year.

English (or hothouse) cucumbers—These come wrapped in plastic and are preferred because they contain a minimal number of seeds and have a thin skin you can always leave on for added nutrition. The common garden cucumber has a thick skin and a considerable core of seeds, and may also taste slightly bitter.

Gem Wraps—All-natural, gluten-free, healthy wraps made of fresh vegetable and fruit purées. These are tasty, vitamin-packed alternatives to bread, tortillas and lavash, and they keep for six months! Soon to be released to national grocery stores, you can also find them online at www.newgemfoods.com.

Gluten-free flours—Wheat flour alternatives are essential to a gluten-free pantry, and there are quite a variety: almond, arrowroot, brown and white rice, buckwheat, chestnut, coconut, corn, cornstarch, garbanzo bean, hazelnut, millet, oat, potato starch, quinoa, sorghum, sweet potato, sweet rice, tapioca and teff flours. All are good choices.

Gluten-free mini bagels, pita bread, taco shells, and tortillas—Good options are widely available in supermarkets and online. Or make your own delicious versions with a variety of gluten-free flours available in natural food stores and online.

Hoisin sauce (gluten-free)—This dark brown, jam-like sauce is made from fermented soybeans flavored with Chinese five-spice powder. It has a pungent, sweet flavor and goes well with pork and beef. It gives a flavor boost to marinades and can be used as a dipping sauce on its own. Lee Kum Kee makes a good one that lasts for up to a year in the fridge.

Nori—These paper-thin sheets are the Big Daddy of seaweeds, dried and used to make traditional sushi for over 1,000 years. These are usually available in 7½ x 8½-inch/19 x 21.6 cm whole sheets and are cut in half to make small sushi rolls.

Origami wraps—The sushi cousin to Gem Wraps, these are dehydrated vegetable- and fruit-based alternatives to traditional seaweed wraps. The colorful, flavorful wraps will totally change how you think about making sushi. They complement a variety of fillings, like ham, cheese, beef and bacon, for your untraditional sushi creations. Super healthy (gluten-free, fat-free, low calorie and full of antioxidants), they add texture and flavor that you have never before seen or tasted.

Rice crumbs—Your best gluten-free alternative to breadcrumbs. Even crunchier than panko. I love these for every need for a crunchy coating.

Rice for sushi—Japanese rice, or *japonica* rice, is a very particular variety. You simply cannot substitute jasmine rice, basmati rice, or other types of long-grain rice because they will not bind and do not share the taste and texture of sushi rice. Seek out the Asian section of most large grocery stores or the local Asian market and ask for sushi rice. "Super-premium short-grain" sushi rice is the best.

Rice noodles—Made from rice flour and water, they have a smooth, chewy texture and also are gluten-free. Fresh ones will be in the refrigerated section of Asian markets, and dried ones will be on the shelves. **Rice sticks** are a dried variation of rice noodles. **Rice vermicelli** is the thin variety of rice noodles.

Rice wrappers (also called rice sheets/skins/spring roll wrappers)—These rice wrappers are dried and come in square or round shapes of different sizes. They are not the same as egg roll wrappers or wonton wrappers, both of which contain wheat flour. Look for them in the Asian section of large supermarkets, at a local Asian market or online.

Salts—You will see one of my three favorites used in most of the recipes: **flake** salt is known for its distinctive pyramid shape, light texture and mild taste; **kosher** salt, as opposed to iodized table salt, has no additives and has larger crystals; **pink** salt, also known as Himalayan salt, is one of the most natural types of salt.

Seasoned rice vinegar—This vinegar is made with sugar and salt. Be careful to read the label since unseasoned rice vinegar (with no sugar or salt) is usually right next to the seasoned ones. (I've grabbed the wrong one a good many times!) Seasoned rice vinegar is added to cooked rice for making sushi but is excellent as salad dressing vinegar as well.

Specialty flours—Gluten-free flours include rice, sweet rice, brown rice, tapioca, sorghum, buckwheat, flaxseed meal and potato starch. All-purpose gluten-free baking flour mixes are also very good.

Sweet Thai chili sauce—This is a thick, sweet-spicy sauce made from ground red chilies, sugar, garlic, vinegar and salt. Don't confuse it with the hotter srirachas—look for the clear, salmon-colored sauce with chili seeds floating in it. It is primarily used as a dipping sauce but also as a glaze for chicken or pork. You can store opened bottles in the fridge for several months.

Tamari sauce—Tamari sauces typically contain only fermented soybeans, and many brands are certified gluten-free. If you're on a gluten-free diet, you should always double-check that you are purchasing a gluten-free tamari. The flavor of tamari is slightly milder than soy sauce, but you can substitute traditional soy sauce for tamari. Use tamari as a dipping sauce, in stir-fries or to give an *umami* flavor to your favorite dishes.

Toasted sesame oil—This amber-colored oil is pressed from roasted sesame seeds and, when used in small quantities, adds a nutty taste that enhances other flavors of a dish and marinades. Opened bottles can be stored at room temperature for several months.

Xanthan gum—A thickening agent for gluten-free baking. It's the "glue" you miss from "glu"-ten.

EQUIPMENT

"You gotta have good gear," is my husband's mantra, and I believe in this doubly for kitchen equipment.

Blenders—Once in your life, go for it and get a good one. It will give your stealth spreads more stealth because the good ones are powerful enough to grind massive amounts of healthy veggies into invisibility. The kids will never see them coming.

Cookie cooling rack—I use these to drain fried foods on because they let air circulate and prevent foods from getting soggy. If you don't want to spend money on a proper cookie cooling rack, just pull one of the baking racks out of the oven and use that.

Cutting boards—A counter-gripping cutting board makes cutting easier and safer. Invest in good quality ones with rubber bumpers to stop slippage and help budding chefs focus on their work. A chef trick, if you don't have bumpers, is to place a wrung-out, wet paper towel underneath your cutting board to anchor it.

Flat-bottomed, fine mesh sieve—A long title for a simple utensil that will make your rice-washing days a breeze. Use to drain washed veggies, fruits and lettuces, too.

Food processors—Invest in a small but good quality one for motoring through a variety of ingredients from chopped nuts to dips, dressings and spreads. A larger one can be used for big batches of sauces and dough-kneading.

Garlic press—One of Mommy's best little kitchen helpers, a press minces garlic in one squeeze without having to touch any garlic.

Graters—From microplane graters, which are excellent for small grating jobs, to the grater attachment on your food processor, which you probably haven't used much, graters are tools you can fall in love with. Get your grater and save as much as 20% on cheese by buying better-tasting blocks of cheddar, Parmesan and Swiss, which you can grate yourself in big batches and keep in the fridge for up to a week.

Mandolin—Another great and inexpensive helper that produces wafer-thin veggies or cheese slices quickly. Use the guard and closely supervise little hands because an effective mandolin is *very* sharp!

Panini press—Great for making compact, warm and gooey sandwiches in a snap without dirtying a skillet. Some waffle makers have a Panini option, too.

Parchment paper or waxed paper—This is the best type of material to wrap many of the rolls because it won't stick to the food as much as plastic wrap and is safer than foil, which can leak or flake off into food. Parchment paper is also great for lining a baking sheet, and either parchment or waxed paper makes a good first layer for double wrapping and freezing sandwiches and burritos.

Pizza stone—For pizzas and pita bread. When the pita dough hits the hot stone it creates steam, which forms the pocket inside pita bread. (If you don't have a pizza stone, turn your thickest baking sheet upside down and use that instead.)

Rice cookers—Cheap ones are fine and do the job, and many brands have brown rice options, too. The more expensive ones can make everything from porridge to risotto, and some even do windows (HA!).

Sauté pans and skillets—A sauté or frying pan has straight sides with a larger bottom surface. They are best for stirring ingredients and searing meats because things are less likely to slop over the sides. A skillet is the pan with slanted sides, perfect for stir-frying and such quick cooking techniques as flipping and sliding things out, like omelets and pancakes.

Sushi rolling mat—These bamboo mats will cost a whopping $2 to $3 and are the key to tight and shapely sushi rolls that will stay intact in lunch boxes.

Y-shaped peelers—The Y-shaped handle is much easier to maneuver (especially if you hold it like a pencil), and the blade is more flexible and effective (code for time-saving!) for thinner slicing, which makes it good for veggie crisps. It will give you none of the frustrating starts and stops of potato peelers.

Rice molds—Super fun for kids to use and easy to find online (also check out "musubi" molds/presses).

Zipper-lock plastic storage bags—Large and small bags are time-savers for everything from storage to marinating to toting chips, fresh fruit, veggies and sammys in lunch boxes. Wash well and re-use to spare the environment.

RESOURCES

STEALTH HEALTH—RECOMMENDED GLUTEN-FREE PRODUCTS

Bob's Red Mill Gluten-Free All-Purpose Rice Crumbs
www.bobsredmill.com

Bob's Red Mill Gluten-Free All-Purpose Baking Flour
www.bobsredmill.com

Glutino Gluten-Free Breadcrumbs
www.glutino.com

Glutino Gluten-Free English Muffins
www.glutino.com

Mission Foods Gluten-Free Corn Tortillas
www.missionfoods.com

Udi's Gluten-Free Bagels
www.udisglutenfree.com

Udi's Gluten-Free Hamburger Buns
www.udisglutenfree.com

Udi's Gluten-Free Pizza Crust
www.udisglutenfree.com

Udi's Gluten-Free Whole Grain Bread Loaf
www.udisglutenfree.com

Katz Gluten-Free Mail Order Bakery
www.katzglutenfree.com

Mariposa Baking Company
www.mariposabaking.com

Trader Joe's
www.traderjoes.com

Wegman's
www.wegmans.com

Whole Foods
www.wholefoodsmarket.com

OTHER SPECIALTY FOOD ITEMS

Gem Wraps and Origami Wraps
www.newgemfoods.com

Asian Food Products (my favorite)
www.uwajimaya.com

ACKNOWLEDGEMENTS

For any creative endeavor it takes, as they say, a village—and this book is no exception. This sushi girl would first like to thank Will Kiester for thinking this book was a good idea. I appreciate your vision and confidence in me. Thank you to Marissa and to the double Megs, B. and P., at Page Street for their patience and good humor. To Coleen, my ever-loving agent: working with you is always delightful. To Danno, whom I forgot to thank the last time, for being the first to encourage me to write a cookbook. To Lindy Moran and the fabulous Little Picasso Studio in Hong Kong, who hosted some happy tastings. You are a sparkling art angel that every kid should get to play with (http://littlepicasso.hk). To Hong Kong International High School's beautiful campus and its great kids. To Ennis Chung for her photo editing, excellent additional photos and long rides to Deep Water Bay. To Leen for helping with everything at the home kitchen. To NewGem Foods, which makes the best wraps in the world—your products make these rolls sing! To Jill, my cohort, coordinator and co-kid wrangler/photographer supreme: you were the bracing organizer that kept me focused and on track. Thank you for always saying, "No problem! That's easy!" To my wonderful husband, Mark, who not only cheered me on every step of the way, but waded through months of photo props, rolls and rice everywhere always with a smile. You are my light and my wings. To all the kids—from New York to L.A., Hong Kong to Korea, and back to New Jersey—who sat patiently through the long tastings and bravely tried some funny-looking food with cameras in their faces—thank you. You made these recipes what they are, and this book is for you all.

INDEX